The Definitive Guide to ImageMagick

Michael Still

Apress®

The Definitive Guide to ImageMagick
Copyright © 2006 by Michael Still

ISBN (Hardback): 1-59059-590-4

Library of Congress Cataloging-in-Publication data is available upon request.

Printed and bound in the United States of America 9 8 7 6 5 4 3 2 1

Lead Editor: Matt Wade
Technical Reviewer: Doug Jackson
Editorial Board: Steve Anglin, Dan Appleman, Ewan Buckingham, Gary Cornell, Tony Davis, Jason Gilmore, Jonathan Hassell, Chris Mills, Dominic Shakeshaft, Jim Sumser
Project Manager: Kylie Johnston
Copy Edit Manager: Nicole LeClerc
Copy Editor: Kim Wimpsett
Assistant Production Director: Kari Brooks-Copony
Production Editor: Linda Marousek
Compositor and Artist: Kinetic Publishing Services, LLC
Proofreader: Kim Burton
Indexer: Carol Burbo
Cover Designer: Kurt Krames
Manufacturing Director: Tom Debolski

Distributed to the book trade worldwide by Springer-Verlag New York, Inc., 233 Spring Street, 6th Floor, New York, NY 10013. Phone 1-800-SPRINGER, fax 201-348-4505, e-mail orders-ny@springer-sbm.com, or visit http://www.springeronline.com.

For information on translations, please contact Apress directly at 2560 Ninth Street, Suite 219, Berkeley, CA 94710. Phone 510-549-5930, fax 510-549-5939, e-mail info@apress.com, or visit http://www.apress.com.

The source code for this book is available to readers at http://www.apress.com in the Source Code section and also at http://www.stillhq.com.

For my ever-patient and loving family—Catherine, Andrew, and Matthew—who put up with me being distracted by random projects, including this one. Thanks to my friends who encouraged me along the way and all those people who asked great questions that I didn't find enough time to answer. I hope your answers are somewhere in here.

Oh, and thanks, Dad, for coming over to provide moral support. What would I have done without you to mind the cat and help me drink all the port? Thanks to Mum as well for all the support during my childhood; it positioned me well to undertake a project like this.

Contents at a Glance

Contents

Foreword

I swear by my life and my love of it that I will never live for the sake of another man, nor ask another man to live for mine.

—John Galt in *Atlas Shrugged*, by Ayn Rand

Like many software projects, ImageMagick lacks good documentation. I designed it to be as intuitive as possible so most users without the benefit of this book could surmise that the following command converts an image in the JPEG format to one in the PNG format:

```
convert image.jpg image.png
```

However, few would realize that the next command turns a flat, two-dimensional label into one that looks three-dimensional with rich textures and simulated depth:

```
convert -background black -fill white -pointsize 72 label:Magick +matte ➡
\( +clone -shade 110x90 -normalize -negate +clone -compose Plus -composite \) ➡
\( -clone 0 -shade 110x50 -normalize -channel BG -fx 0 +channel -matte \) ➡
-delete 0 +swap -compose Multiply -composite button.gif
```

ImageMagick has been in development for nearly 20 years, and for 20 years users of the project have rightly complained about its lack of documentation. I have never had the opportunity to write a book, because I am perpetually consumed with answering ImageMagick questions, fixing bugs, and adding enhancements. So when Matt Wade from Apress approached me about writing a book on ImageMagick, I did the proverbial happy dance.

Apress did well finding Michael Still to present ImageMagick to you. I know of Michael because of some articles he wrote on ImageMagick for IBM DeveloperWorks. I often refer ImageMagick users to those articles when they want a gentle introduction to using ImageMagick from the command line.

ImageMagick started with a request by my DuPont supervisor, Dr. David Pensak, to display computer-generated images on a monitor capable of showing only 256 unique colors simultaneously. In 1987, monitors that could display 24-bit true-color images were rare and quite expensive. There were a plethora of chemists and biologists at DuPont but few computer scientists to confer with. Instead, I turned to Usenet for help and posted a request for an algorithm to reduce 24-bit images to 256 colors. Paul Raveling of the USC Information Sciences Institute responded with not only a solution, but one that was already in source code and available from his FTP site. Over the course of the next few years, I had frequent opportunities to get help with other vexing computer science problems I encountered in the course of doing my job at DuPont. Eventually, I felt compelled to give thanks for the help I received from the knowledgeable folks on Usenet. I decided to freely release the image-processing tools I developed to the world so that others could benefit from my efforts.

In 1990 few freely available image-processing tools existed, so I expected an enthusiastic reception. Before a release was possible, Dr. Pensak had to convince upper management at

DuPont to give away what they might have perceived as valuable intellectual property. I suspect they agreed simply because ImageMagick was not chemically or biologically based, so they did not understand its value to the company. Either way, ImageMagick would not be available today without DuPont's permission to distribute it. ImageMagick was posted to Usenet's comp.archives group on August 1, 1990.

After ImageMagick's release, I got the occasional request for an enhancement, a report of a bug, or a contribution to the source base. In the mid-1990s, I released the culmination of these efforts, ImageMagick 4.2.9. At the time, I thought ImageMagick was complete. Thousands of folks worldwide were using it, and it was even showing up as part of a new operating system being distributed freely called Linux.

The next generation of ImageMagick, version 5, started when Bob Friesenhahn contacted me and began suggesting ways to improve it. Bob had seemingly boundless energy, questions, and ideas. He suggested I revamp ImageMagick 4.2.9, so in addition to the command-line tools, it should have a usable application programming interface (API) so users could leverage the image-processing algorithms from other languages or scripts. Bob also wrote a C++ wrapper for ImageMagick called Magick++ and began contributing enhancements such as the module loader facility, automatic file identification, and test suites. In the meantime, the project picked up a few other notable contributors: Glenn Randers-Pehrson, William Radcliffe, and Leonard Rosenthol. By now, ImageMagick was being utilized by tens of thousands of users, who reacted gruffly when a new release broke an existing API call or script. The other members of the group wanted to freeze the API and command line, but I was not quite ready, since ImageMagick was not quite what I had envisioned it could be. Bob and others created a fork of ImageMagick called GraphicsMagick. I alone continued to develop ImageMagick.

I did not work alone for long. Anthony Thyssen contacted me about deficiencies in the ImageMagick command-line programs. He pointed out that the command line was confusing when dealing with more than one image. He suggested an orderly, well-defined method for dealing with the command line, and this became ImageMagick 6 (the current release). His efforts are detailed at his Web pages, Examples of ImageMagick Usage, at http://www.cit.gu.edu.au/~anthony/graphics/imagick6/. In addition to this book, I highly recommend you peruse his site. He has illustrated the power of ImageMagick in ways even I did not know were possible.

It has been nearly 20 years since ImageMagick was first conceived, and it looks likely that it will be here for another 20 and beyond. The command line and the API are stable, but there is still work to do. We're currently working on improving the Scalable Vector Graphics (SVG) support and adding better support for video formats. And, of course, I always have questions from the community to keep me busy. In fact, I better get back to work—while I was writing this foreword I received several e-mails with ImageMagick questions. I am grateful that in the future, I'll be able to answer most ImageMagick questions simply by pointing people to this book.

Cristy
Principal ImageMagick Architect
November 2005

About the Author

MICHAEL STILL has been working on imaging applications for eight years and has been programming for many more. His interest in imaging applications started with his employment at IPAustralia, the Australian patent, trademark, and designs office, where he was tasked with modifying an open source PDF-generation library to support TIFF images. This developed into a long-term series of projects using custom imaging code and ImageMagick to implement a line of business systems.

During this time, Michael was responsible for imaging databases, including a database of nine million TIFF files for the Australian Patent Office and a database of all images associated with trademarks in Australia. He also wrote his Panda PDF-generation library, as well as a variety of other open source imaging tools, in this time. You can find his open source code at `http://www.stillhq.com`.

Michael has written a number of articles on ImageMagick for IBM DeveloperWorks (`http://www.ibm.com/developer/`). He has also presented at a variety of conferences and was previously the maintainer of the `comp.text.pdf` frequently asked questions (FAQ) document.

Michael has recently accepted a job with Google as a systems administrator. His experience involves developing large-scale systems, performing systems administration of vertical systems (many of which he developed), and solving other interesting-sounding engineering problems. His previous employer was TOWER Software, developers of a leading Electronic Document and Records Management (EDRM) product, where he worked on imaging problems, as well as a variety of server functionality, including several Web-based products.

About the Technical Reviewer

DOUG JACKSON has worked in the IT industry since 1985 in fields ranging from hardware design, communications, programming, systems administration, and IT security to project management and consulting. During this time, he has become fluent in a number of programming languages, including C/C++, Java, Assembler, and Forth, on both Microsoft and Unix systems. Doug first encountered ImageMagick in 1997 while writing large-scale image-processing and image-viewing software for the Australian Patent Office.

When Doug isn't being an information security consultant, he enjoys teaching the fine art of sailing to Cub Scouts, playing guitar, and solving hardware puzzles with PIC microprocessors. He is married to Megan, arguably the most wonderful and patient lady on the planet, and has two terrific daughters (Cate and Siân).

Acknowledgments

It always seemed corny to me that authors thank the usual suspects for helping with the production of their book. They normally thank the publisher's editorial team, their families, and perhaps their workmates. My problem is that I now discover these sentiments are genuinely true.

If it weren't for Matt Wade initially contacting me and pitching the project, I wouldn't have ever started. If it weren't for the able assistance of Tina Nielsen and my project manager, Kylie Johnston, the project would have faltered along the way. If it weren't for the able review of the manuscript by Doug Jackson and Matt Wade, then this book's content would have suffered. There is also, of course, the layout team, which has produced such a wonderful-looking finished project, especially Linda Marousek, who was my contact point with that team.

Then there's my family, who have gone out of their way to make my life easier while writing the book. Be it leaving Daddy alone for a bit to hack on some sample code or just understanding when I was dazed and confused after a day of writing—thanks, Catherine, Andrew, and Matthew.

My workmates were instrumental, too; without the encouragement of Gordon Taylor, Anthony Drabsch, Simon Dugard, Chris Crispin, Grant Allen, and Lindsay Beaton, I probably wouldn't have let Matt talk me into writing the book.

Andrew Pollock deserves a special mention for providing the hosting for my site and the blog for this book. Many thanks for your patient support and advice.

I want to save two final special acknowledgments to last—Kim Wimpsett was my copy editor, and I never imagined that having my own personal English grammar coach would be such fun. American English isn't my first language (I'm an Australian, and we do English the British way, which is of course better), and I didn't appreciate all the subtle differences until Kim helped me out. The book flows better and makes more sense because of Kim's input.

Finally, this book would have nothing to talk about if it weren't for Cristy and all the other contributors to ImageMagick over the years. ImageMagick is an incredibly deep product, which makes it wonderful to write about. The efforts to which the team has gone to make a product that works cannot be underestimated. Cristy recommended Anthony Thyssen, Bob Friesenhahn, Glenn Randers-Pehrson, and William Radcliffe as being instrumental in the development of ImageMagick and thus deserving of my thanks. Thanks, guys.

I'm sure I've forgotten to thank some people here, and I apologize to them for that. Thanks, folks.

Introduction

The ideal reader of this book is someone with immediate imaging needs who is prepared to either use command-line tools or use the ImageMagick programmer's interface to write code. Many of the concepts demonstrated are also available in the ImageMagick graphical tools, but almost all the examples in this book focus on the command-line tools.

This book provides hundreds of working examples of how to use ImageMagick for everyday problems, as well as the theory necessary to understand what's happening in those examples. I recommend you install ImageMagick before reading this book so you can work along with the examples provided. (Chapter 1 covers how to install ImageMagick for the first time.)

How This Book Is Structured

This book starts by describing how to install ImageMagick on your system and then covers how to configure it. After that, I launch into covering the ImageMagick command-line tools. Complete coverage isn't possible, however, because ImageMagick is so rich. After I've covered the command-line tools, I show working examples of four applications developed with some of the ImageMagick APIs.

The chapter breakdown is as follows:

Chapter 1, "Installing and Configuring ImageMagick": Chapter 1 discusses how to install and configure ImageMagick on Microsoft Windows and Unix machines, including how to install binary versions, what those packages are likely to be called in your Linux distribution, and how to compile ImageMagick from source on both Unix and Microsoft Windows operating systems.

Chapter 2, "Performing Basic Image Manipulation": Chapter 2 covers simple image manipulations such as resizing, sample, cropping, scaling, thumbnailing, and so forth. This chapter contains information about all the ImageMagick transformations used to create smaller or larger versions of an image. To discuss these topics, the chapter also introduces the differences between raster and vector image formats and how raster formats are encoded.

Chapter 3, "Introducing Compression and Other Metadata": In Chapter 3, I discuss compression options for image files, show how to use ImageMagick to change the compression used for a file, and provide recommendations about which file format to use in various scenarios. I'll also discuss file formats that can contain more than one image per file, show how to handle animations, and discuss the metadata you can associate with image files.

Chapter 4, "Using Other ImageMagick Tools": Chapter 4 covers the various other ImageMagick tools that aren't covered extensively in the rest of the book. Five chapters in the book cover the `convert` command; this chapter covers the others: `compare`, `composite` (previously known as `combine`), `conjure`, `identify`, `import`, `mogrify`, `montage`, `animate`, and `display`. The rationale behind the focus on the `convert` command is that most of the functionality offered by these commands in this chapter can also be accessed via `convert`.

Chapter 5, "Performing Artistic Transformations": Chapter 5 is my chance to show off the more artistic transformations that ImageMagick can apply; these include blurring images, adding charcoal effects, imploding images, adding noise to images, making an image look like it was painted by hand, adding beveled edges, creating shadows, spreading pixels randomly, and so forth.

Chapter 6, "Performing Other Image Transformations": Finally for the command-line image transformations, there is Chapter 6. This chapter mops up all the command-line operations that haven't been demonstrated in earlier chapters, apart from those used to draw or annotate images (which are covered in the next chapter). These operations are the more routine of those offered by ImageMagick, such as adding borders, rotating images, manipulating contrast in the image, dithering an image, and so on.

Chapter 7, "Using the Drawing Commands": Chapter 7 is the last chapter that documents the `convert` command. In this chapter, I discuss how to create and annotate images using the drawing commands that ImageMagick implements. Also, I discuss how to specify colors and then walk you through each of the drawing and annotation commands available.

Chapter 8, "PerlMagick: ImageMagick Programming with Perl": Chapter 8 is the first of the programming chapters, and it covers a Web photo management system written in Perl using the PerlMagick ImageMagick interface.

Chapter 9, "Implementing Your Own Delegate with C": ImageMagick implements support for new image formats with delegates. This chapter demonstrates how to write a simple delegate to support your own image format using the C programming language.

Chapter 10, "RMagick: ImageMagick Programming with Ruby": Chapter 10 demonstrates a simple command-line interface to build batch conversion jobs written in Ruby. The code allows you to interactively apply ImageMagick operations to an image and then apply all the operations you used on that image to all the images in a specified directory with a specified filename filter.

Chapter 11, "MagickWand: ImageMagick Programming with PHP": Chapter 11 demonstrates a PHP implementation of an on-the-fly graph-generation page using ImageMagick. The graphs use image composition to provide nice-looking output.

Chapter 12, "Where to Go from Here": The final chapter of the book covers those final little issues that are always handy to know, such as where to find information about topics not covered in this book, how to join the ImageMagick community, and how to report bugs.

Prerequisites

This book discusses ImageMagick 6.2.3. The concepts discussed are applicable to future and previous releases, however. Further, the book's content is relevant regardless of the platform on which ImageMagick is installed.

You can download ImageMagick from its Web site at http://www.imagemagick.org.

Contacting the Author

You can e-mail Michael Still at imagemagick@stillhq.com, and you can find his Web site at http://www.stillhq.com. You can find the ImageMagick blog for the book at http://www.stillhq.com/imagemagick/, and you can find the Apress page for the book at http://www.apress.com/book/bookDisplay.html?bID=10052.

For all the examples in this book, the figures are available online at http://www.apress.com in the Source Code section and at http://www.stillhq.com/imagemagick/book/. The online figures are full-color images, so you can download them if you need to further understand an example.

CHAPTER 1

■■■

Installing and Configuring ImageMagick

This chapter will give you detailed instructions on how to obtain, install, and configure ImageMagick. It also will discuss the architectural design of ImageMagick and explain how you can use that architecture to expand and customize ImageMagick. Finally, it will discuss how to get online help and debug problems you might have with ImageMagick.

If you already have ImageMagick installed on your machine, then you can skip the "Installing Precompiled Versions" and "Installing from Source" sections of this chapter.

Installing Precompiled Versions

By far the quickest and easiest way to install ImageMagick is to install the precompiled binary version, which is probably packaged by either your operating system provider or the ImageMagick team. Too many Linux distributions exist to cover all of them here, so I have limited this discussion to the two main packaging formats—apt and RPM.

If your chosen operating system isn't covered in this chapter, then fear not—you have two options for installing ImageMagick. First, it's quite possible that your operating system provider has packaged ImageMagick, so you should check in the normal place for your operating system. Second, failing that, you can refer to the "Installing from Source" section of this chapter to install ImageMagick from source. To do this, you'll need a compiler installed on your machine, though.

Debian and Ubuntu Linux

On both Debian and Ubuntu Linux, the name of the package to install is imagemagick. I personally run Debian Unstable on my laptop, and this installed, until recently, the same version of ImageMagick that Ubuntu 5.04 (Hoary Hedgehog) installs, which is 6.0.6. This is quite old compared with the latest version of ImageMagick at the time of writing of this book, which is 6.2.3.

Debian Unstable has now upgraded to the latest upline ImageMagick, so you should see that new version flow through to the next release of Ubuntu as well.

Red Hat Linux

Fedora Core 3 has packaged ImageMagick as well. The name of the package to install is ImageMagick, and when I did a default install, it was already installed on the system, which was nice. The version of ImageMagick currently packaged with Fedora Core 3 is 6.0.7, which is a little out of date.

Older ImageMagick Versions

As discussed in the previous sections, several of the more common Linux distributions currently install older versions of ImageMagick by default. You can cope with this problem in a couple of ways. The first option is that you could of course just download the source for ImageMagick and compile and install it yourself. You'll find instructions on how to do that later in the "Installing from Source" section if you're interested. Another option is to find someone else who has compiled the latest version and has already packaged it for your chosen distribution. Instructing you on how to do this, however, is outside the scope of this book. Finally, you should find that most of the features discussed in this book also work with the older versions of ImageMagick that are still shipping.

Microsoft Windows

Installing ImageMagick on Microsoft Windows machines is fairly trivial. The first step is to download the installer from http://www.imagemagick.org. You'll find a link to the download page on the left side of the home page. Download the installer, and run it. Figure 1-1 shows the first screen you'll see.

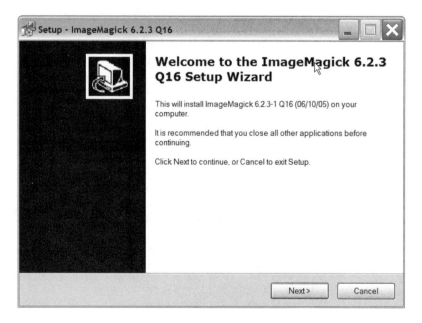

Figure 1-1. *Viewing the welcome screen for the installer*

The installer recommends that you close all other applications that are running on the machine before proceeding, which is a fairly common requirement. I recommend you do indeed do this, which will minimize the risk of ending up in an inconsistent state with the dynamic link libraries (DLLs) on your system. Click Next. You're now presented with a screen that asks you to agree with the license agreement for ImageMagick, which is something you'll need to do for any of the versions discussed in this chapter. Figure 1-2 shows a sample of what this screen looks like.

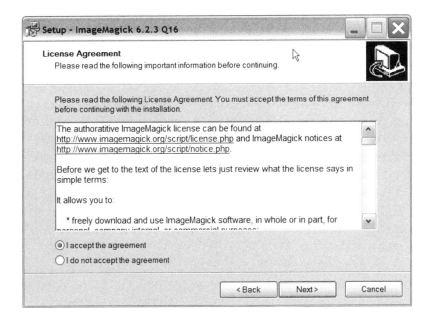

Figure 1-2. *Reading the ImageMagick license agreement*

If you do agree with the license agreement, then select Accept the Agreement, and then click Next. If you don't accept the agreement, then ImageMagick will not be installed. Next, you'll see a screen explaining some of the administrative requirements of the installation. If you've previously installed a version of ImageMagick and are attempting to upgrade instead of having two versions side by side on the machine, then you'll need to uninstall that version before proceeding with the installer, as shown in Figure 1-3. Additionally, if you want to install ImageMagick so that any user on the machine can use it, then you'll need to run the installer from the Administrator account. Remember, however, that older versions of Microsoft Windows don't necessarily have the concept of an Administrator account, which means that all users of the machine will get ImageMagick by default.

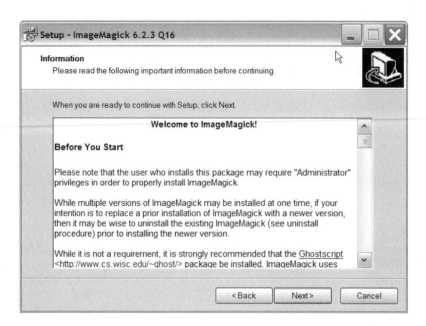

Figure 1-3. *Getting some reminders about the install process*

After clicking Next, you'll be asked where to install ImageMagick on your disk, as shown in Figure 1-4. I like selecting the default here so that all my applications are together in the `Program Files` directory, but if you're low on disk space on one partition, then you can install ImageMagick to another partition.

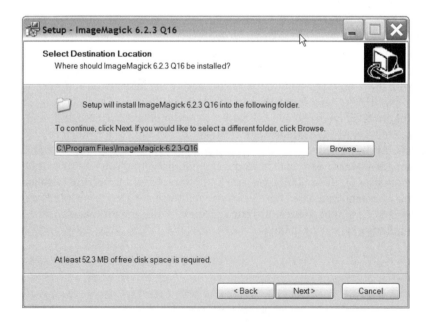

Figure 1-4. *Selecting the directory in which to install ImageMagick*

After clicking Next, you'll be asked for the name of the folder in the Start ➤ Programs menu for Windows. The default name is pretty sensible, but you can change it if you want, as shown in Figure 1-5.

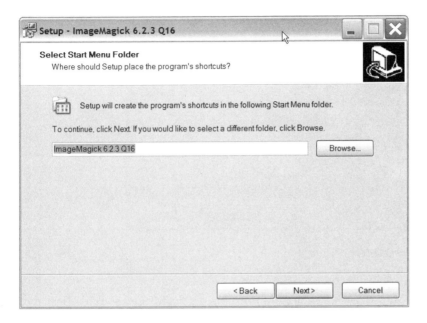

Figure 1-5. *Selecting a name for the entry in the Programs menu*

After you click Next, the subsequent screen asks questions about the rest of the install process. Note that if you want to use ImageMagick from the command line, as discussed in most of this book, then you're best off updating the executable search path so that the Windows command shell can find the ImageMagick executables. I've also chosen to use ImageMagick as my viewer, so I associated the file extensions, which isn't the default, as shown in Figure 1-6.

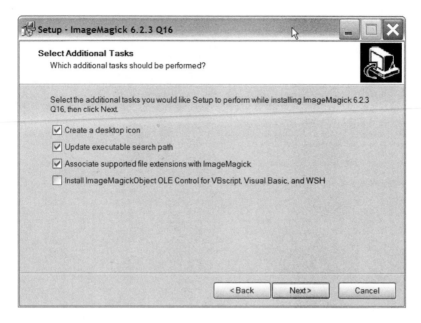

Figure 1-6. *Selecting installation options*

ImageMagick's installer now has enough information to proceed. After you click Next, the installer will show you the final configuration screen, which confirms the installation settings, as shown in Figure 1-7.

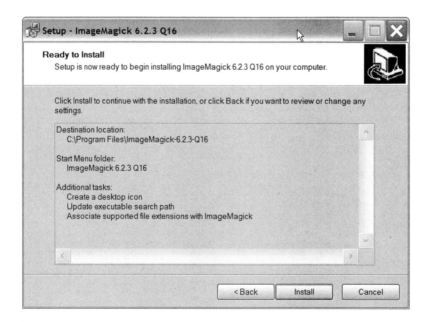

Figure 1-7. *Confirming installation settings*

Click Install to start the installation. You'll see a progress bar, as shown in Figure 1-8, even though the install doesn't take long (at least on my machine).

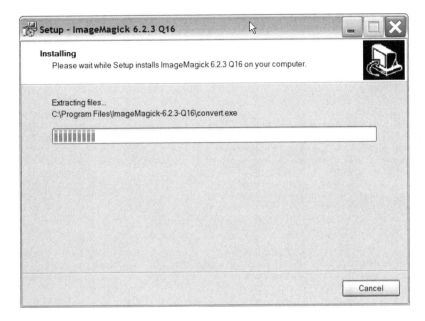

Figure 1-8. *Watching the installation progress*

The installer now provides some advice about how to make sure your installation worked, as shown in Figure 1-9. I recommend you follow these instructions, because if the installation has failed, then you'll be confused when you try to work along with the examples in the book and they don't work.

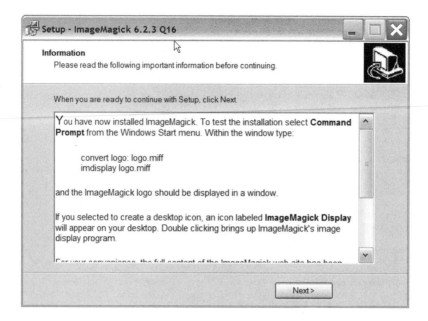

Figure 1-9. *Reviewing information about how to test the ImageMagick installation*

The final screen in the installer offers to take you to the ImageMagick documentation, as shown in Figure 1-10. Uncheck the box if you don't want the documentation to open in your default browser.

Figure 1-10. *Do you want to see some documentation?*

You've now installed ImageMagick for Microsoft Windows and tested the installation, so you're set to go.

Installing from Source

If a packaged version of ImageMagick for your operating system doesn't exist, or if you want more control over configuring and installing ImageMagick, then you might consider installing the software from source. The following sections of the chapter outline how to do this, but it's important to remember that I will assume that you already have a compiler installed and working on your machine. Depending on the operating system, this might mean you need to purchase compiler software from your vendor or install an open source alternative.

Introducing Dependencies

You'll need to install a number of dependencies in addition to ImageMagick in order to have a fully functional ImageMagick installation. It's important that these dependencies are installed before you start configuring and compiling ImageMagick, because the `configure` script for ImageMagick will disable functionality that isn't available because of missing dependencies at compile time.

In other words, if `libpng` (which is needed for supporting the PNG image format) were missing at the time that you ran the `configure` script, then this functionality would be missing from your ImageMagick installation. This is true even if you installed `libpng` after compiling ImageMagick. In that case, you'd need to reconfigure and recompile ImageMagick for the new functionality to become available.

Several classes of dependencies exist, each of which is discussed in turn in the following sections.

Introducing Delegates

For some of its work, ImageMagick uses command-line tools called *delegates* to encode and decode the image file in a format that ImageMagick can use. That intermediate format can then be further processed before being saved into the format that you want. This means the ImageMagick team can implement significantly fewer file format conversion routines without losing any functionality. You can see an example of the delegate detection process in the section "Compiling on Unix Operating Systems." You can also add your own delegates to the mix by using the delegate configuration file, which is discussed in the "Using Configuration Files" section. Chapter 9 also contains an example of a custom delegate.

For now, I'll stick to listing the delegates that ImageMagick supports so that you know what you might want to install before you compile ImageMagick from source (see Table 1-1).

Table 1-1. *Delegates Used by ImageMagick*

Delegate Name	Used For	URL to Download the Delegate From
bzlib	Bzip compression in MIFF files	`http://sources.redhat.com/bzip2/`
DPS	Display PostScript, which is used only for Postscript files if Ghostscript is unavailable	

(Continued)

Table 1-1. *(Continued)*

Delegate Name	Used For	URL to Download the Delegate From
FlashPIX	FlashPIX format	`ftp://ftp.imagemagick.org/pub/ImageMagick/delegates/libfpx-1.2.0.9.tar.gz`
FreeType	TrueType fonts	`http://www.freetype.org`
GhostPCL	PCL page description language	`http://www.artifex.com/downloads/`
Ghostscript	PostScript and PDF document formats	`http://www.cs.wisc.edu/~ghost/`
Graphviz	Graphviz visualization	`http://www.graphviz.org`
JBIG	JBIG lossless, black-and-white compression format	`http://www.cl.cam.ac.uk/~xml25/jbigkit/`
JPEG	JPEG files	`ftp://ftp.uu.net/graphics/jpeg/jpegsrc.v6b.tar.gz`
JPEG 2000	JPEG 2000 files (the next version of the JPEG compression standard)	`http://www.ece.uvic.ca/~mdadams/jasper/`
LCMS	ICC CMS color management	`http://www.littlecms.com/`
PNG	Support for the PNG image format	`http://www.libpng.org/pub/png/pngcode.html`
TIFF	Support for the TIFF image format	`http://www.libtiff.org`
WMF	Support for Windows metafiles	`http://sourceforge.net/projects/wvware/`
zlib	Support for deflate compression	`http://www.gzip.org/zlib/`

Each of these delegates is open source and can be separately downloaded and installed before ImageMagick is configured if you need the facilities it implements. Details for how to install each of these dependencies is outside the scope of this chapter, but each of these delegates comes with excellent documentation about how to perform the installation steps needed.

Compiling on Unix Operating Systems

The following instructions apply to Linux, the various BSDs (including FreeBSD, OpenBSD, and NetBSD), Solaris, Mac OS X, AIX, and many other Unix variants. ImageMagick is identical to most other open source projects in its installation methodology. For those of you who haven't done this before, don't worry, because I'll walk you through the process.

The first step is to download the source code from the ImageMagick Web site at `http://www.imagemagick.org`. On the current site, the download link is on the left side of the screen and leads you to a page where you can download the source code.

Once you have the source code, you'll need to uncompress it. As I mentioned earlier, the current version of ImageMagick at the time of writing this book is 6.2.3, so that's what I'll use in these examples. Anyway, here's how to decompress the source code:

```
tar -xvzf ImageMagick.tar.gz
```

You should see output like this:

```
ImageMagick-6.2.3/
ImageMagick-6.2.3/Install-mac.txt
ImageMagick-6.2.3/depcomp
ImageMagick-6.2.3/ImageMagick.spec.in
ImageMagick-6.2.3/PerlMagick/
ImageMagick-6.2.3/PerlMagick/Makefile.PL
ImageMagick-6.2.3/PerlMagick/Makefile.nt
ImageMagick-6.2.3/PerlMagick/.gdbinit
ImageMagick-6.2.3/PerlMagick/Makefile.PL.in
ImageMagick-6.2.3/PerlMagick/Makefile.am
ImageMagick-6.2.3/PerlMagick/demo/
ImageMagick-6.2.3/PerlMagick/demo/Turtle.pm
ImageMagick-6.2.3/PerlMagick/demo/lsys.pl
ImageMagick-6.2.3/PerlMagick/demo/demo.pl
ImageMagick-6.2.3/PerlMagick/demo/tree.pl
ImageMagick-6.2.3/PerlMagick/demo/shapes.pl
ImageMagick-6.2.3/PerlMagick/demo/yellow_flower.gif
ImageMagick-6.2.3/PerlMagick/demo/Generic.ttf
ImageMagick-6.2.3/PerlMagick/demo/composite.pl
ImageMagick-6.2.3/PerlMagick/demo/red_flower.gif
ImageMagick-6.2.3/PerlMagick/demo/steganography.pl
ImageMagick-6.2.3/PerlMagick/demo/smile.gif
ImageMagick-6.2.3/PerlMagick/demo/shadow_text.pl
ImageMagick-6.2.3/PerlMagick/demo/annotate.pl
ImageMagick-6.2.3/PerlMagick/demo/src.png
ImageMagick-6.2.3/PerlMagick/demo/Makefile
...
```

The output shown here from that command is an example of what you'll see. I've truncated the listing here because it would fill several pages and not be particularly interesting to read.

Note You can find out more about the tar command, and the arguments it takes, by reading the tar man page. If manual pages have been installed on your system, you can access the man page by typing man tar. If manual pages aren't installed, then you'll find many examples of them online.

Now that you've extracted the source code, change directories into the new source code directory that tar extracted for you, and configure the code, like so:

```
cd ImageMagick-6.2.3
./configure
```

The name of the directory will change if you've extracted a different version of ImageMagick. The output from the tar command will tell you the directory name, however. You'll see output like this:

```
configuring ImageMagick 6.2.3
checking build system type... i686-pc-linux-gnu
checking host system type... i686-pc-linux-gnu
checking target system type... i686-pc-linux-gnu
checking whether build environment is sane... yes
checking for a BSD-compatible install... /usr/bin/install -c
checking for gawk... gawk
checking whether make sets $(MAKE)... yes
checking for gcc... gcc
checking for C compiler default output file name... a.out
checking whether the C compiler works... yes
checking whether we are cross compiling... no
checking for suffix of executables...
checking for suffix of object files... o
checking whether we are using the GNU C compiler... yes
checking whether gcc accepts -g... yes
checking for gcc option to accept ANSI C... none needed
checking for style of include used by make... GNU
checking dependency style of gcc... gcc3
checking how to run the C preprocessor... gcc -E
checking for a sed that does not truncate output... /bin/sed
checking for egrep... grep -E
checking for ld used by gcc... /usr/bin/ld
checking if the linker (/usr/bin/ld) is GNU ld... yes
checking whether gcc and cc understand -c and -o together... yes
checking for a BSD-compatible install... /usr/bin/install -c
checking whether make sets $(MAKE)... (cached) yes
checking maximum warning verbosity option...  -Wall for C
checking whether ln -s works... yes
checking for gcc... (cached) gcc
checking whether we are using the GNU C compiler... (cached) yes
checking whether gcc accepts -g... (cached) yes
checking for gcc option to accept ANSI C... (cached) none needed
checking dependency style of gcc... (cached) gcc3
checking if malloc debugging is wanted... no
...
```

Again, I've truncated the output so as to not fill the entire book with command output. I'll show the last few lines from the output, though, because they're important:

```
ImageMagick is configured as follows. Please verify that this configuration
matches your expectations.

Host system type : i686-pc-linux-gnu
```

```
                   Option                         Value
--------------------------------------------------------------------------
Shared libraries   --enable-shared=yes            yes
Static libraries   --enable-static=yes            yes
Module support     --with-modules=no              no
GNU ld             --with-gnu-ld=yes              yes
Quantum depth      --with-quantum-depth=16        16

Delegate Configuration:
BZLIB              --with-bzlib=yes                      no
DPS                --with-dps=yes                        no
FlashPIX           --with-fpx=no                         no
FreeType 2.0       --with-ttf=yes                        yes
GhostPCL           None                                  pcl6 (unknown)
Ghostscript        None                                  gs (8.01)
Ghostscript fonts --with-gs-font-dir=default    /usr/share/ghostscript/fonts/
Ghostscript lib    --with-gslib=no                       no
Graphviz           --with-dot=yes                        no
JBIG               --with-jbig=yes                       no
JPEG v1            --with-jpeg=yes                       yes
JPEG-2000          --with-jp2=yes                        no
LCMS               --with-lcms=yes                       no
Magick++           --with-magick-plus-plus=yes  yes
PERL               --with-perl=yes                       /usr/bin/perl
PNG                --with-png=yes                        yes
TIFF               --with-tiff=yes                       yes
Windows fonts      --with-windows-font-dir=      none
WMF                --with-wmf=yes                        no
X11                --with-x=                              yes
XML                --with-xml=yes                        yes
ZLIB               --with-zlib=yes                       yes

X11 Configuration:
  X_CFLAGS     = -I/usr/X11R6/include
  X_PRE_LIBS   = -lSM -lICE
  X_LIBS       = -L/usr/X11R6/lib
  X_EXTRA_LIBS =

Options used to compile and link:
  PREFIX      = /usr/local
  EXEC-PREFIX = /usr/local
  VERSION     = 6.2.3
  CC          = gcc
  CFLAGS      = -g -O2 -Wall -pthread
  CPPFLAGS    = -I/usr/local/include
  PCFLAGS     =
  DEFS        = -DHAVE_CONFIG_H
  LDFLAGS     = -L/usr/local/lib -L/usr/X11R6/lib -lfreetype -lz -L/usr/lib
```

```
LIBS        = -lMagick -ltiff -lfreetype -ljpeg -lpng -lXext -lXt -lSM ➥
-lICE -lX11 -lxml2 -lz -lpthread -lm -lpthread
CXX         = g++
CXXFLAGS    = -pthread
```

This dump shows all the features that ImageMagick has found available on your system and is going to enable during the compile. It also shows you features that might be interesting to you depending on your technical bent, such as the compiler it has decided to use, and so forth. Checking this list is important, because it tells you what features will not be available because of missing dependencies.

The center column of the table contains command-line options you can use to force an option that's otherwise enabled or disabled to be set to a given state. For example, let's say you already know that the JBIG library is installed on this machine and you don't want TIFF support for some reason (such as wanting to produce a smaller executable for an embedded application). To achieve this, just run the configure script like this:

```
./configure --with-jbig --without-tiff
```

If the configure script can't find JBIG support, then it still won't be enabled, whereas TIFF support will be disabled by this command. The next step is simply to compile ImageMagick, like so:

```
make
```

Now you just need to install the compiled code, which you can do with this command:

```
make install
```

This final command is the only one that requires you to have administrative permissions on your computer because it installs to privileged areas of the system.

Installing Using FreeBSD Ports

Installing on the FreeBSD platform is simple if done through the ports tree. It's highly recommended that you use the ports tree unless you have some need for a custom compilation of ImageMagick. When using the ports tree, all the dependencies are taken care of for you.

First, you should make sure you have a working, up-to-date ports tree. The ImageMagick port is located in the /usr/ports/graphics/ImageMagick directory. The standard configuration is most likely fine for you, unless you happen to know that you need to modify the configure-line arguments. If you do need to pass in configure arguments, you can browse through the Makefile to see which arguments exist. To install ImageMagick, simply go to the directory, and run the proper installation command, like so:

```
cd /usr/ports/graphics/ImageMagick
make install distclean
```

When new versions of ImageMagick are released, you'll want to upgrade your installation. In FreeBSD, you can do this in a variety of ways, but it's recommended to install the portupgrade package to handle all your upgrade needs:

```
cd /usr/ports/sysutil/portupgrade
make install distclean
```

Once you have the `portupgrade` package installed, you can check for any out-of-date packages with the following command:

```
/usr/local/sbin/portversion | grep '<'
```

Any out-of-date packages will be displayed as follows:

```
courier-imap              <
gettext                   <
glib                      <
ImageMagick               <
```

To update a package, use the `portupgrade` command as such:

```
/usr/local/sbin/portupgrade ImageMagick
```

Compiling ImageMagick on Microsoft Windows

It's possible that you'll want to install ImageMagick from source code on a Microsoft Windows system. This section gives step-by-step instructions on how to make that happen. I've used Microsoft Visual Studio 2003 for this section, because it's the currently released version of Microsoft's C compiler. By the time you hold this book in your hands, it's probable that Microsoft Visual Studio 2005, and the associated Visual Studio Express versions, will have been released. The compilation instructions for those compilers should be identical to the steps presented here.

Note The Visual Studio Express products are free versions of the full Microsoft Visual Studio product. The difference is that they are low cost, they support only one language each (and are therefore smaller downloads), and they aren't meant to be used to develop commercial software. They should be fine for compiling open source applications such as ImageMagick, though. You can find out more information about them at `http://lab.msdn.microsoft.com/express/`.

The first step is to download the source code from `http://www.imagemagick.org`. You'll find a link to the download page on the left side of the page. Once you've uncompressed the source code you downloaded, you next need to configure the project files for ImageMagick. The ImageMagick source download provides a wizard that helps with this process; however, before you can run the wizard, you need to compile it.

The source download for the latest version of ImageMagick was intended to be compiled with Microsoft Visual Studio 2002 (also known as Visual Studio 7). This isn't a big problem, because Visual Studio will upgrade the project files for you, but it does mean you'll be prompted to make sure this is what you want to do. The prompt looks like Figure 1-11.

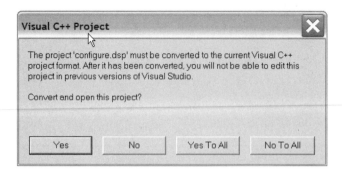

Figure 1-11. *Visual Studio 2003 will prompt for permission to upgrade the project file.*

Click Yes at this prompt. Now select the release build target, and compile the code by selecting Build ➤ Build Solution. After a successful compilation, you should see the output in the Output pane at the bottom of the screen. Figure 1-12 shows of a version of that dockable pane.

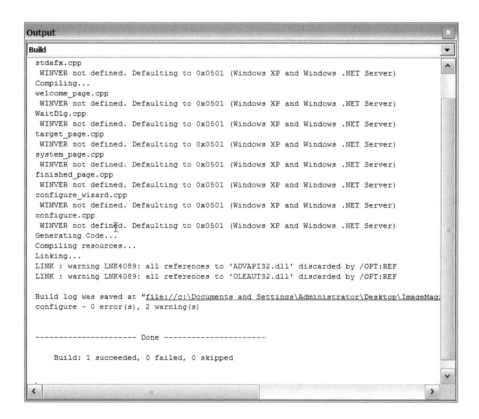

Figure 1-12. *Output from a successful compilation of the configuration wizard*

If your compilation has a build failure listed, then you'll need to investigate what caused the wizard to fail to compile, which is outside the scope of this chapter. Once you've compiled the wizard, you can run it. You can either do this from Windows Explorer or just run the application within Visual Studio by selecting the Debug ➤ Start Without Debugging menu command.

Figure 1-13 shows the first screen of the wizard.

Figure 1-13. *The first screen of the source configuration wizard*

This first screen greets you with the configuration wizard and lets you know that the purpose of the configuration wizard is to create project files for the various components of ImageMagick to allow for compilation to occur. Click Next, and you're presented with the Target Setup dialog box, as shown in Figure 1-14.

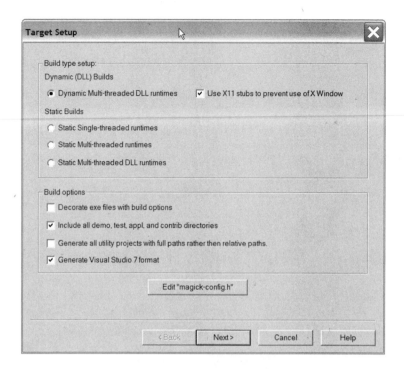

Figure 1-14. *Configuring the ImageMagick project files*

A lot is happening in this window, so let's work through each topic one at a time:

Dynamic versus static binaries: A lot of the dialog box is dedicated to selecting whether you want a dynamic or static binary. Dynamic binaries use DLLs to hold all the contributed libraries in a modular manner. This means that other applications can also use those libraries, and you don't need to store multiple copies of the library on disk. In return, you'll occasion-ally get naming and version conflicts. Static binaries are just one big executable, and all the library code is moved into that one .exe file. This means the application is easier to move to other machines and isn't going to stop working if someone else upgrades a DLL, but you might end up in a situation where more disk space is used in return.

Single versus multithreaded runtimes: How many people are going to be using ImageMagick at once? If you're ever going to want to have more than one operation occurring within ImageMagick at once, then select multithreaded runtimes.

Using X11 stubs to prevent the use of X Window: X Windows is the windowing system used on Unix machines. If you compile with the X11 stubs, then ImageMagick won't attempt to integrate with the X server that you're probably not running on your Microsoft Windows machine. Several ImageMagick commands don't work without an X server, though, as discussed in Chapter 4.

Decorating .exe *files with build options*: If you've defined a different set of build options, you can pass these onto the executable files. Given you're not doing that, leave this option unchecked.

Including all demonstration, contributed, and test executables directories: You can compile the demonstration, contributed, and test executables as well. (Leave this option checked for now.)

Generating all utility projects with full paths rather than relative paths: You can configure whether the utility projects care about the exact path they're located at or just the path relative to the top-level project.

Generating Visual Studio 7 format project files: Check the Generate Visual Studio 7 Format box, because it will make upgrading the project files to Visual Studio 2003 easier later.

Editing the magick-config.h *header file*: Finally, a button allows you to edit the magick-config.h header file if you'd like. This isn't needed for a simple compile, and you should refer to the compilation instructions that ship with ImageMagick if necessary.

After clicking Next, you'll see the System Setup dialog box, as shown in Figure 1-15.

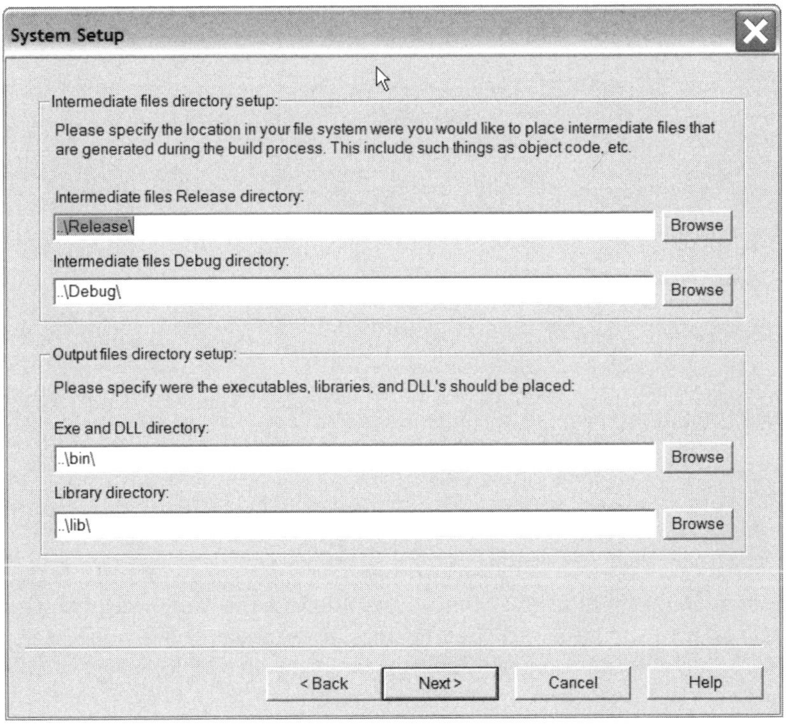

Figure 1-15. *Configuring the ImageMagick output directories*

If you need to, you can change where the compiled files are placed via this dialog box. The defaults are reasonable, however, so I didn't change them for my compile. You get one final window from the wizard, as shown in Figure 1-16.

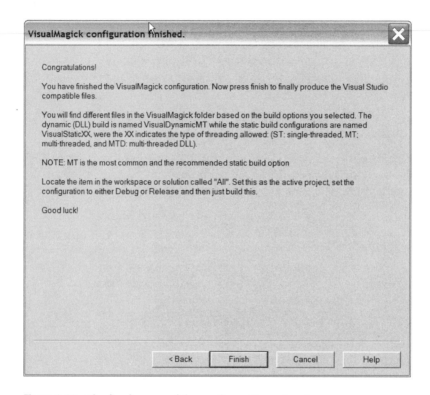

Figure 1-16. *The final screen of the configuration wizard*

The wizard has created a solution file (the file with the `.sln` extension) for the options you have selected, which will be at the top level of the source directory. My source directory looks like Figure 1-17.

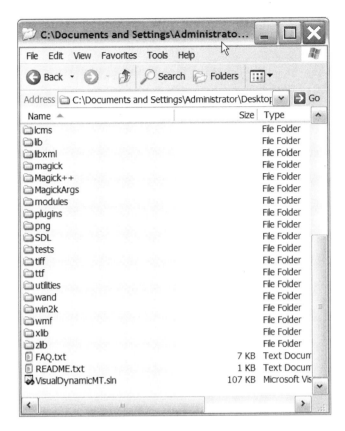

Figure 1-17. *The generated solution file*

Open the solution file, and you'll once again be prompted to upgrade the projects to the Visual Studio 2003 format, as shown in Figure 1-18.

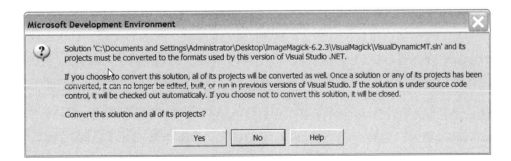

Figure 1-18. *Upgrading the project files to the Visual Studio 2003 format*

Click Yes here. Now find the project named "All" in the Solution Explorer, which is on the right side of the screen by default. Right-click that project, and select Set As Startup Project from the menu. Now select Build ➤ Build Solution, and the compile will start.

The compile will take a little while, depending on the speed of your machine. On my 1.7-gigahertz Intel Centrino laptop, the compile took about six minutes. At the end of my compile, I get the Output pane shown in Figure 1-19.

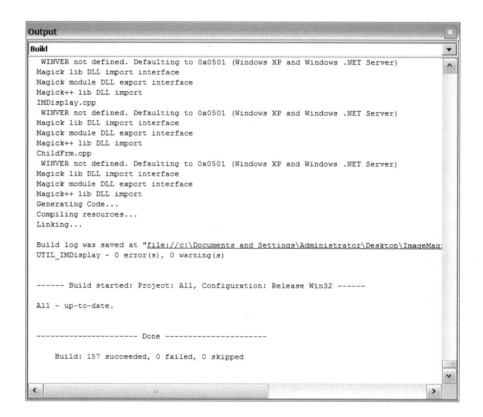

Figure 1-19. *The Output pane after compilation*

If no failures are listed in the Output pane, then you'll have a compiled version of ImageMagick in the output directory you specified in the configuration wizard.

Exploring the Architecture of ImageMagick

ImageMagick consists of a series of components. These components fall into two overall categories—modules and delegates. *Modules* are ImageMagick's code for handling a given image format. When a dependency isn't available at compile time, then that module will be disabled. *Delegates* are an extremely similar concept, but delegates are also extensible. You'll notice that I've already discussed delegates when showing how to compile from source. The "Introducing Delegates" section covered the delegates that ship by default with ImageMagick. Refer to the next section, "Using Configuration Files," for more information on adding delegates to ImageMagick, and to Chapter 9, which discusses how to write a simple delegate of your own in C.

You can configure ImageMagick in two more ways. The method I've already discussed is of course using the various compilation options that are available when you build from source. The two additional ways of configuring ImageMagick are using configuration files and using environment variables, each of which is covered in its own section.

Using Configuration Files

ImageMagick is really quite configurable. I won't spend a lot of time on the contents of the configuration files, because ImageMagick includes excellent documentation on the inner workings of the configuration files. However, Table 1-2 points you in the right direction and gives you some idea of the features you can configure with ImageMagick.

Table 1-2. *ImageMagick Configuration Files*

Configuration File	Configures
coder.xml	The association between image formats and the encoder/decoder module for that format.
colors.xml	Lets you specify the name of a color and define its red, green, blue, and alpha values. For example, perhaps you want a color named "bernard." Here is the place to define what that color actually is. Chapter 7 discusses colors in more depth.
configure.xml	Build parameters.
delegates.xml	Here you can specify your own custom delegates for image formats that ImageMagick didn't originally know about.
english.xml	Associates message tags with a given English string.
locale.xml	The same as english.xml but for other locales.
log.xml	Configures logging.
magic.xml	Many file formats are identified by a "magic number" at the start of the file. This configuration file lets you map a new magic number to a given image format.
type.xml	Configures fonts.
type-ghostscript.xml	Configures Ghostscript fonts.
type-windows.xml	Configures Microsoft Windows fonts.

Where these configuration files are located changes depending on how ImageMagick was installed and depending on your operating system. Check the following three sections to see where the configuration files are located on your system. Finally, if ImageMagick can't find the configuration files at all, then it will use the built-in default values.

Location of Configuration Files for Source Installations

The configuration files are located in a directory on disk. Some of these locations refer to the installation prefix as $PREFIX, which is where ImageMagick was installed. It's usually /../usr/local/ on a Unix machine when installing from source. ImageMagick checks the following locations, in this order, looking for these configuration files:

1. The location defined by the `MAGICK_CONFIGURE_PATH` environment variable (see the "Using Environment Variables" section)

2. `$PREFIX/lib/ImageMagick-6.2.3/config`

3. `$PREFIX/share/ImageMagick-6.2.3/config`

4. `$PREFIX/share/ImageMagick-6.2.3`

5. A folder named `.magick` in the current user's home directory

6. A folder in the client path with the name `lib/ImageMagick-6.2.3`

7. The current directory

Location of Configuration Files for Binary Installations

If the ImageMagick installation was done from a binary package, then the following search order is used, where the environment variable `MAGICK_HOME` should have been set to the location of the ImageMagick installation:

1. The location defined by the `MAGICK_CONFIGURE_PATH` environment variable (see the "Using Environment Variables" section)

2. `$MAGICK_HOME/lib/ImageMagick-6.2.3/config`

3. `$MAGICK_HOME /share/ImageMagick-6.2.3/config`

4. `$MAGICK_HOME /share/ImageMagick-6.2.3`

5. A folder named `.magick` in the current user's home directory

6. A folder in the client path with the name `lib/ImageMagick-6.2.3`

7. The current directory

Location of Configuration Files on Microsoft Windows

The configuration locations are a little different on Microsoft Windows. If you're running on Microsoft Windows, then the configuration files will be in one of these locations, which are searched in the following order:

1. The location defined by the `MAGICK_CONFIGURE_PATH` environment variable (see the "Using Environment Variables" section)

2. The location defined by the `MAGICK_HOME` environment variable

3. A folder named `.magick` in the current user's home directory

4. A folder in the client path with the name `lib/ImageMagick-6.2.3`

5. The current directory

Using Environment Variables

ImageMagick also supports a number of environment variables to control its behavior. These environment variables are defined in the user's shell and affect only the operation of ImageMagick programs started from that shell. Many system administrators will configure these environment variables in a user's shell profile, however, which means that every interactive shell will be initialized with them.

Instead of including the full list of environment variables in this chapter, I recommend you refer to the ImageMagick documentation if you want to configure the behavior of ImageMagick further.

Limiting Resource Usage on the Command Line

It's also possible to limit the resource usage such as disk and memory that ImageMagick consumes while performing a given command. You can do this with the `limit` command-line option, which can limit the following parameters:

- `Area`

- `Disk`

- `File`

- `Map`

- `Memory`

Each of these limits is a number. In the case of disk and memory limits, you can use the text `MB` to symbolize megabytes.

Determining What Is Configured

If you need to determine on a machine that you didn't configure, or configured some time ago, what modules, delegates, and so forth, are configured, then use the `list` command. The `list` command takes the following arguments:

- `Coder`

- `Color`

- `Delegate`

- `Format`

- `Magic`

- `Module`

- `Resource`

- `Type`

For example, to see which delegates are configured on my machine, I can type the following:

```
convert -list delegate
```

I get the following output for this command:

Path: /usr/lib/ImageMagick-6.2.3/config/delegates.xml

Delegate	Command
cgm =>	ralcgm" -d ps -oC < "%i" > "%o" 2>/dev/null
crw =>	/usr/bin/dcraw" -3 -w -c "%i" > "%o"
dcr =>	/usr/bin/dcraw" -3 -w -c "%i" > "%o"
dvi =>	dvips" -q -o "%o" "%i
emf =>	wmf2eps" -o "%o" "%i
eps<=>pdf	gs" -q -dBATCH -dSAFER -dMaxBitmap=500000000 -dNOPAUSE ➥ -dAlignToPixels=0 -sDEVICE="pdfwrite" -sOutputFile="%o" -f"%i
eps<=>ps	gs" -q -dBATCH -dSAFER -dMaxBitmap=500000000 -dNOPAUSE ➥ -dAlignToPixels=0 -sDEVICE="pswrite" -sOutputFile="%o" -f"%i
fig =>	fig2dev" -L ps "%i" "%o
gplt =>	echo" "set size 1.25,0.62
	set terminal postscript portrait color solid; ➥
	set output "%o";
	load "%i"" > "%u";"gnuplot" "%u
hpg =>	hp2xx" -q -m eps -f `basename "%o"` "%i
	mv -f `basename "%o"` "%o
hpgl =>	if [-e hp2xx -o -e /usr/bin/hp2xx]; then
	hp2xx -q -m eps -f `basename "%o"` "%i
	mv -f `basename "%o"` "%o
	else
	echo "You need to install hp2xx to use HPGL files with ➥
	ImageMagick.
	exit 1
	fi
htm =>	html2ps" -U -o "%o" "%i
html =>	html2ps" -U -o "%o" "%i
https =>	@WWWDecodeDelegateDefault@" -q -O "%o" "https:%i
ilbm =>	ilbmtoppm" "%i" > "%o
man =>	groff" -man -Tps "%i" > "%o
miff<= win	/usr/bin/display" -immutable "%i
mrw =>	/usr/bin/dcraw" -3 -w -c "%i" > "%o"
nef =>	/usr/bin/dcraw" -3 -w -c "%i" > "%o"
orf =>	/usr/bin/dcraw" -3 -w -c "%i" > "%o"
pdf<=>eps	gs" -q -dBATCH -dSAFER -dMaxBitmap=500000000 -dNOPAUSE ➥ -dAlignToPixels=0 -sDEVICE="epswrite" -sOutputFile="%o" -f"%i
pdf<=>ps	gs" -q -dBATCH -dSAFER -dMaxBitmap=500000000 -dNOPAUSE ➥ -dAlignToPixels=0 -sDEVICE="pswrite" -sOutputFile="%o" -f"%i
pnm<= ilbm	ppmtoilbm" -24if "%i" > "%o
pnm<= launch	gimp" "%i
pov =>	povray" "+i"%i"" +o"%o" +fn%q +w%w +h%h +a -q9 -kfi"%s" -kff"%n
	convert" -concatenate "%o*.png" "%o

```
ps<=>eps        gs" -q -dBATCH -dSAFER -dMaxBitmap=500000000 -dNOPAUSE ➡
                -dAlignToPixels=0 -sDEVICE="epswrite" -sOutputFile="%o" -f"%i
ps<=>pdf        gs" -q -dBATCH -dSAFER -dMaxBitmap=500000000 -dNOPAUSE ➡
                -dAlignToPixels=0 -sDEVICE="pdfwrite" -sOutputFile="%o" -f"%i
ps<= print      lpr "%i
rad =>          ra_ppm" -g 1.0 "%i" "%o
raf =>          /usr/bin/dcraw" -3 -w -c "%i" > "%o
rgba<= rle      modify" -flip -size %wx%h "rgba:%i
                rawtorle" -w %w -h %h -n 4 -o "%o" "%i
scan =>         scanimage" -d "%i" > "%o
shtml =>        html2ps" -U -o "%o" "%i
txt<=>ps        enscript" -o "%o" "%i
wmf =>          wmf2eps" -o "%o" "%i
x3f =>          /usr/bin/dcraw" -3 -w -c "%i" > "%o
```

Using ImageMagick

Now that you have ImageMagick installed and configured, you should know some final useful points before getting going with the rest of the book. The following sections discuss accessing online help, debugging output, creating verbose output, and determining which version of ImageMagick is installed on a machine.

Online Help

The first way of finding out how to perform an action with ImageMagick is to check the online help. This is especially useful if you're trying to do something you've done before but you can't quite remember the syntax for the command. On Unix systems, ImageMagick comes with quite a large set of man pages, which can be accessed with the man command. A good place to start is by looking at the following:

```
man imagemagick
```

Depending on the system, you might also have Hypertext Markup Language (HTML) documentation installed at /usr/share/doc/ImageMagick. Start with the index.html file, and navigate from there. For Microsoft Windows, the documentation is installed by default and appears in the ImageMagick folder under Start ➤ Program Files. This same documentation is available online at http://www.imagemagick.org.

If you're just wondering what the arguments to a given command-line option are, or what the name of a command-line option is, then you can also try the help command-line option, like so:

```
convert -help
```

This lists all the command-line options supported by that ImageMagick utility and provides a one-line description of each.

Debug Output

ImageMagick provides extensive debugging output if you add the debug command line to the command you're executing. For example, to convert a PNG file to a JPEG file, you execute the following command:

```
convert input.png output.jpg
```

You'll find out more about this command in Chapter 2 and Chapter 3. If you want to see what ImageMagick is doing when it performs this conversion, then just add the debug command to the command line:

```
convert -debug input.png output.jpg
```

You'll get a lot of output, which traces the execution of ImageMagick. This debugging output shows the internal execution of ImageMagick and can be handy if you think you've found a bug and need to make a bug report.

If you want to disable all debug output, then use the +debug command instead:

```
convert +debug input.png output.jpg
```

This can be useful when the global system configuration turns on debugging output but you don't want it for a specific command. Finally, you can specify the format of the debugging output by using the log command-line option. For more information on the options available here, refer to the ImageMagick online help, as discussed previously.

Verbose Output

If you want to know what's happening inside ImageMagick when your command is being executed but you don't want the extreme level of logging that you get with debug output, then consider asking for verbose output instead. Again, if the original command were this:

```
convert input.png output.jpg
```

then the verbose version of this command would be this:

```
convert -verbose input.png output.jpg
```

This will give you the following output:

```
input.png PNG 666x487 666x487+0+0 DirectClass 27kb 0.020u 0:01
input.png PNG 666x487 666x487+0+0 DirectClass 27kb
TIFF Directory at offset 0x0
  Image Width: 666 Image Length: 487
  Resolution: 47.24, 47.24 pixels/cm
  Bits/Sample: 8
  Compression Scheme: AdobeDeflate
  Photometric Interpretation: RGB color
  FillOrder: msb-to-lsb
  Document Name: "output.tif"
  Orientation: row 0 top, col 0 lhs
  Samples/Pixel: 3
  Rows/Strip: 487
  Planar Configuration: single image plane
  Software: ImageMagick 6.2.3 06/09/05 Q16 http://www.imagemagick.org
  Predictor: horizontal differencing 2 (0x2)
input.png=>output.tif PNG 666x487 666x487+0+0 DirectClass 21kb 0.200u 0:01
```

Here you can see that ImageMagick believes it has taken a PNG image that's 666 pixels wide and 487 pixels high and has converted it to a TIFF file. You even get a dump of the TIFF directory (what a TIFF image calls the header for the image itself) that ImageMagick wrote into output.tif.

What Version of ImageMagick Is Installed?

Finally, it can occasionally be useful to know which version of ImageMagick is running on a given machine. You can find this out with the version command-line option. Here's an example from my laptop:

```
convert -version
```

This gives the following results:

```
Version: ImageMagick 6.2.3 06/09/05 Q16 http://www.imagemagick.org
Copyright: Copyright (C) 1999-2005 ImageMagick Studio LLC
```

So, you can see that on my laptop I have 6.2.3 Q16 installed.

Conclusion

This chapter hasn't been the most exciting chapter that you'll read in the book, but it's an important one, because it shows you how to get ImageMagick installed on your machines. Now that you have ImageMagick installed, you can move onto the much more interesting aspects of ImageMagick, such as Chapter 2, which talks about changing the size of images and making thumbnails; Chapter 3, which talks about how to convert images between different compression formats; and Chapter 5, which shows how to apply some fantastic visual effects to your images.

If you need more details for the instructions in this chapter, then I recommend you refer to Chapter 12, which covers more details about how to get help online, where the various ImageMagick community resources are, and where to find the Web site for this book, which is where I'll post any errata and changes to the build process as I learn about them.

■■■

## CHAPTER 2

Performing Basic Image Manipulation

This chapter will give you some basic examples of how to use ImageMagick. Since this is really your first exposure to ImageMagick as a tool, it's useful to take it a little slower here and learn the basics well.

Probably the most useful tool to ship with the ImageMagick suite is the convert command; it lets you convert images between various compression formats and implement some useful and visually pleasing transformations. You can find a list of the file formats that ImageMagick supports at http://www.imagemagick.org/script/formats.php. Chapter 3 covers how to convert between image formats.

In this chapter, I'll cover the common operations that you're likely to want to use ImageMagick for: resizing images, filtering images, cropping images, and trimming images. This chapter will introduce the ImageMagick suite and how to use the various commands that perform these operations.

Because I'm introducing the tools for the first time in this chapter, the chapter will go through the steps more slowly than the rest of the book, so don't be dismayed that the book seems to spend a large amount of time on seemingly obvious things—the pace will improve once these introductory features are out of the way.

So, you'll now see all the useful manipulations you can do with the ImageMagick suite.

Introducing Imaging Theory

Before you can transform images, you need to be aware of some imaging theory. I'll introduce only the minimum to get you going here, and then I'll cover new pieces of theory throughout the rest of the book when they're needed. If you want to find out about a specific piece of theory later, then just look it up in the index.

If you're comfortable with the concept of vector and raster images, the difference between these two types of image format, and pixels, then feel free to skip to the "Changing the Size of an Image" section of this chapter. If you're not familiar with these, then read on—you'll learn about them now.

The single theoretical factor that affects the quality of results you'll achieve in this chapter the most is *pixelation*, which is when an image becomes blocky and jagged. At a basic level, a computer has two ways of storing pictures: vector images and raster images. The different picture styles are really for quite different tasks, and ImageMagick is much more suited to working with raster images than vector images. Vector images won't suffer from pixelation problems, however.

I'll now describe the two image formats in turn.

Vector Images

Imagine that you take a piece of paper and start to free draw a picture. The picture comprises straight lines that form simple shapes such triangles, squares, rectangles; curves including circles, and so forth; letters that form words; and other such basic picture elements. Figure 2-1 shows an example of a simple vector image.

Figure 2-1. *A sample vector image*

Ignoring the relative lack of artistic merit in the picture, you can see that it consists of a series of relatively simple graphical elements—straight lines, curves, and so forth. Each element of the picture is stored individually in the vector file as a mathematical description. In fact, the following is a snippet of the picture if it's stored in a vector format called Scalable Vector Graphics (SVG):

```
<?xml version="1.0" encoding="UTF-8" standalone="no"?>
<!DOCTYPE svg PUBLIC "-//W3C//DTD SVG 1.0//EN" ➥
"http://www.w3.org/TR/2001/PR-SVG-20010719/DTD/svg10.dtd">
<svg width="19cm" height="14cm" viewBox="4 3 19 14">
  <ellipse style="fill: #ffffff" cx="8.46874" cy="7.5" rx="3.46874" ry="3.46874"/>
  <ellipse style="fill: none; fill-opacity:0; stroke-width: 0.2; stroke: #000000" ➥
cx="8.46874" cy="7.5" rx="3.46874" ry="3.46874"/>
  <ellipse style="fill: none; fill-opacity:0; stroke-width: 0.02; stroke: #000000" ➥
cx="8.46874" cy="7.5" rx="3.46874" ry="3.46874"/>
  <line style="fill: none; fill-opacity:0; stroke-width: 0.2; stroke: #000000" ➥
x1="8" y1="6" x2="8" y2="7"/>
  <line style="fill: none; fill-opacity:0; stroke-width: 0.2; stroke: #000000" ➥
x1="9" y1="6" x2="9" y2="7"/>
  <path style="fill: none; fill-opacity:0; stroke-width: 0.2; stroke: #000000" ➥
d="M 7,8 A 1.625,1.625 0 0 0 10,8"/>
```

```
<polygon style="fill: #ffffff" points="16,7.5 18.3333,7.03333 17.1667,5.16667 ➡
19.0333,6.33333 19.5,4 19.9667,6.33333 21.8333,5.16667 20.6667,7.03333 23,7.5 ➡
20.6667,7.96667 21.8333,9.83333 19.9667,8.66667 19.5,11 19.0333,8.66667 ➡
17.1667,9.83333 18.3333,7.96667 "/>
```

You can see here that each element is described in terms of the shape's fill, the starting coordinates, the ending coordinates, the stroke thickness, and the color.

Therefore, because the picture is described in terms of mathematical formulae, it can be scaled to any set of size dimensions without losing any of the image quality. This is the technology that operating system vendors introduced with fonts such as PostScript and TrueType—you can resize the fonts to any size, and they will look good because the description can render at any size.

Vector graphics are not the solution to all problems, however. A lot of information, such as photographs and scanned images, cannot be represented well with vector graphics. For example, how would you turn a picture of a tree from your camera into a set of lines and so forth? You can try, but it would take a lot of time and processing effort and probably would not look that good.

Raster Images

The other option for storing image information is raster images. Imagine that you drew the smiley face from Figure 2-1 on graph paper and insisted that the lines consisted of just colored squares on the grid paper. A square also needs to be colored or not colored—you have no option to only half color a square (although anti-aliasing does offer some compromises here, as discussed in Chapter 7). You'd end up with a picture more like Figure 2-2.

Figure 2-2. *A rasterized version of the smiley face from the vector version in Figure 2-1*

Again, you'll have to forgive me for my lack of talent at drawing pictures. You can see here that the image is a lot blockier than in Figure 2-1. This is because the image has been expanded so that you can see the individual squares on the grid paper. Those squares are called *pixels*. (You'll learn more about this "blockiness" in images when they're made larger in the "Making an Image Larger" section.)

Now look at some pixels from a real photo; Figure 2-3 shows the photo of a tree that was taken on a digital camera and therefore is a raster image.

Figure 2-3. *A photo of a tree*

If you zoom in on some of the pixels in the image, then they become a lot clearer, as shown in Figure 2-4.

Figure 2-4. *Zooming in on some of the pixels from Figure 2-3*

The set of colored squares to the right of the photo is a close-up of the pixels in the small box on the right side of the photo (near the top of the branches of the tree). You can see that the pixels in the raster image provide only an approximation of what the camera was actually pointed at, because a set number of samples makes up the image. The most important way that this will impact you as a user of images is that raster images are generally larger files on disk and a lot harder to resize.

I've covered enough theory for now, so the next section covers how you can start to perform some useful tasks with ImageMagick. The rest of this chapter deals solely with raster images, because resizing vector images is much easier than resizing the more common raster format.

Invoking convert

The only other key point you need to know before changing the size of an image is how to invoke the convert command line that you'll use throughout the examples in this chapter. The basic invocation of convert is to pass the name of the input file and then the name of the output file. So, if you wanted to convert a JPEG image into a PNG image (these compression formats are discussed in more detail in Chapter 3), you'd use the following command line:

```
convert input.jpg output.png
```

Unless there is an error, this command won't return any output to the command line but will produce a new file named output.png, which has the same image as input.jpg but in PNG format.

Changing the Size of an Image

Probably the most common transformation that you can perform on an image is to resize it. Whether it's taking the large images from your digital camera and making them a smaller size for display on your Web site or it's making thumbnails of those same images for the index pages of your photo gallery, resizing is something that happens to images all the time.

The convert command provides several ways to resize an image. Each of them does it in a slightly different way, and each is used in a slightly different scenario, so I'll cover them one at a time in the following sections. To work through the examples, I'll provide a simple usage scenario for each instance to demonstrate when you'd use that technique.

Making an Image Smaller

Let's say you just took the picture shown in Figure 2-5 with your digital camera, and now it's time to post it online. It's a nice full-resolution image, because you want one day to be able to do some pretty exciting things with the pictures you take, such as printing full-sized posters and projecting them onto walls in your home or office.

Figure 2-5. *A sample photograph for resizing*

I took this photo a while ago on a 2-megapixel camera, so posting it online wasn't a big problem, although I did make it smaller so that it would fit on the smaller monitors that many members of my family used at the time. With today's 8-megapixel and higher cameras, however, each picture can be more than 20 megabytes if not compressed. Clearly, if you post this image on a Web site, you would need to make it smaller so that the download time isn't excessive. Compression is the other factor that greatly affects the size of an image file. (Chapter 3 covers the details surrounding compression.)

Another factor to take into account is that halving the length of each of the sides of a raster image will reduce the uncompressed size of the image by 75 percent. This is best described diagrammatically, as shown in Figure 2-6.

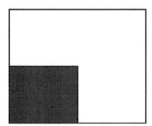

Figure 2-6. *The effect of reducing the length of the sides of a rectangle*

You can see here that if you reduce the length of each of the sizes by half, then the total area of the rectangle ends up being a quarter of the previous value. This quite drastically reduces the size of the image file. Table 2-1 shows some real-world data to back up that statement.

Table 2-1. *Comparative Sizes for a Photo*

Photo Resolution (Width×Height)	File Size (JPEG Compressed)
2,560×1920	2.2 megabytes
1,280×960	784 kilobytes
640×480	280 kilobytes
320×240	112 kilobytes
160×120	56 kilobytes
80×60	36 kilobytes

You can also see from Table 2-1 that the advantage of reducing the size of an image in terms of side length compared with file size on disk decreases as the image gets smaller. For example, reducing the side length from 160×120 pixels to 80×60 pixels reduces the size of the file by less than 50 percent, whereas reducing the side length from 2560×1920 to 1280×960 reduces the size of the file by about 70 percent. Figure 2-7 shows a graph of that in action.

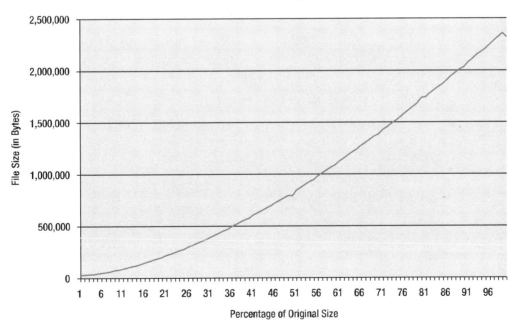

Figure 2-7. *The effect on file size of varying the length of the sides of an image*

Interestingly, you can also see that reducing the dimensions of the image by a small margin results in a larger file size. This is probably because the JPEG compression algorithm doesn't handle the new file size as well as the original one because it is not a multiple of 8 pixels wide.

Anyway, now that you know why it's desirable to resize images, let's assume you want to reduce the size of some pictures so that you can post them on your Web site. I'll use the picture from Figure 2-5 for the following examples. ImageMagick's `convert` command supports several ways of performing this resizing operation. Not surprisingly, one of those commands is `resize`.

Resizing an Image

The first way of changing the size of an image that I'll discuss is the `resize` option to the `convert` command. This option takes a specification for the new size and then operates on the images that are also passed to `convert`. Most of the ImageMagick commands behave in this manner—the command-line options are executed in order during the conversion from the input file to the output file. This means you can have more than one conversion occur at any one time.

The `resize` option offers a few ways to specify the new size for the image:

Absolute size: You can specify the exact size of output image you want by using pixels. The first number is the new width of the image, and the second number is the new height of the image. The following example code resizes an image to be 42×148 pixels. You need to be careful of this option, however, because it will change the *aspect ratio* of the image. The aspect ratio is the ratio between the horizontal and vertical edges, and if it changes, you'll often end up with an image that is noticeably distorted. To change the size but keep it in proportion with the original, you must use numbers that are multiples of the original.

```
convert -resize 42x148 input.jpg output.jpg
```

Percentage change: You can specify the new size as a percentage of the old size. For example, the following command line results in an image that is 12.5 percent of the previous size of the image. This version of the dimensions will maintain the current aspect ratio.

```
convert -resize 12.5% input.jpg output.jpg
```

Maximum area: This method allows you to specify the maximum area (width multiplied by height) that the image can consume. ImageMagick will pick side lengths for the image that are in the same ratio as the original image and that are as large as possible while not exceeding the specified maximum area.

```
convert -resize 1000@ input.jpg output.jpg
```

The original image here is a 1,280×960-pixel, compressed JPEG photograph. After the `resize` command has run, the output image is a 36×27-pixel image. This makes an image with an area of 972 pixels, which means it doesn't exceed the specified maximum. Because the aspect ratio of the sides was maintained, if you divide 1,280 by 36, or 960 by 27, you'll get the same number, in this case 35.5555556.

Maximum image dimensions: You can specify the maximum size for an image, and the image will be resized only if its dimensions exceed that specification. For example, the following command line will resize only those images bigger than 640×480 pixels, in which case you'll get an image that is 640×480 pixels.

```
convert -resize 640x480< input.jpg output.jpg
```

Minimum image dimensions: Similarly, by changing the less-than sign to a greater-than sign, you can specify that all images should have at least a certain minimum set of dimensions. The following example ensures that the image has at least dimensions of 640×480 pixels. If the image is smaller than this, then it will be made bigger so that it has dimensions of 640×480 pixels. For more discussion on the issues associated with making images larger, see the "Making an Image Larger" section later in this chapter.

```
convert -resize 640x480> input.jpg output.jpg
```

Negation of minimum and maximum sizes: It is also possible to negate the logic applied for the minimum and maximum size operators discussed in the two previous points by placing an exclamation mark before the greater-than or lesser-than sign. This inverts the logic applied for that operation.

Resampling an Image

Another way of resizing an image is called *resampling*. Resampling is interesting in that it doesn't change the size of the image; it changes the resolution of the image. So, for example, if you have an image that is two inches wide and three inches high at 100 dots per inch, then it will be 200×300. If you resample the image to 300 dots per inch, then you'll change the image to be 600×900 pixels.

The observed size of the image won't change, though. You'd use this conversion so that the image would print and display correctly on devices with varying resolutions. For example, most monitors are 75 dots per inch, and most printers are at least 600 dots per inch. Here's an example of the resample command-line option at work:

```
convert -resample 300x300 input.tif output.tif
```

Only a few image formats store the current image resolution inside the image file itself—TIFF, PNG, and JPEG are the three most common. If the image format you're using doesn't store the image resolution, you can specify it with the density command-line option (discussed in Chapter 3). You should also note this caveat from the ImageMagick documentation, however:

> *Note that Photoshop stores and obtains image resolution from a proprietary embedded profile. If this profile exists in the image, then Photoshop will continue to treat the image using its former resolution, ignoring the image resolution specified in the standard file header.*

Filtering an Image

When an image is resized, *filtering* (the process of determining which pixels make it into the new image and what color they are) needs to occur to decide what the new image will look like. Take the case of making an image smaller. In this case, more than one pixel affects the value of one pixel in the output image. Figure 2-8 shows an example of an image before any filtering has occurred.

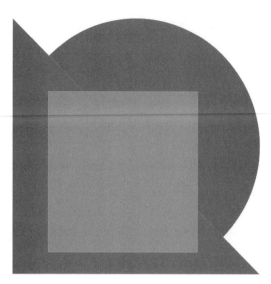

Figure 2-8. *A simple input image*

If you take this relatively simple image and make it a fair bit smaller, then each pixel in the new image will be the average of a number of pixels in the original image. Figure 2-9 shows a zoomed-in version of the process that will make this clearer.

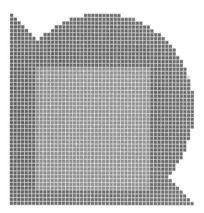

Figure 2-9. *A zoomed-in look at a simple image after it has been made smaller*

You can see here that the edges of the circle are a lot rougher than they were in the original image, because the averaging process hasn't been very forgiving.

ImageMagick offers several *filters*, all of which will perform best in certain specific situations:

- Point
- Box
- Triangle
- Hermite
- Hanning
- Hamming
- Blackman
- Gaussian
- Quadratic
- Cubic
- Catrom
- Mitchell
- Lanczos
- Bessel
- Sinc

ImageMagick applies a reasonable default filter, normally Lanczos, if you don't specify one. The differences between these various filters are quite technical and outside the scope of this book. You can learn more about these filters at Anthony Thyssen's excellent ImageMagick tutorial at `http://www.cit.gu.edu.au/~anthony/graphics/imagick6/resize/#filters`. You specify a filter with ImageMagick as follows:

```
convert -sample 400% -filter lanczos input.jpf output.jpg
```

This example creates an output file that has dimensions four times greater than those of the input and uses the Lanczos filter to guess what the new pixel values should be.

Scaling an Image

If you have specified a filter and you don't want it to apply, then you can use the `scale` command-line option. It functions the same as the `resize` command but ignores the `filter` option if specified. It also ignores any gravity specified. (You'll read more about gravity in Chapter 7.) The `scale` option also uses a simpler, faster scaling algorithm, which might be useful if you're processing a lot of images.

Here's an example of how to use the `scale` command-line option:

```
convert -filter quadratic -scale 300% input.jpg output.jpg
```

Sampling an Image

The sample command-line option is the same as the resize command-line option, but the filter argument is again ignored. sample uses a more complex algorithm than scale and is therefore slower but sometimes produces nicer results. If you want to change the size of the image but either don't want to specify a filter or want to not use the filter that you've specified, then use the sample command-line option.

Here's an example of how to use the sample command-line option:

```
convert -filter quadratic -sample 640x480 input.jpg output.jpg
```

Creating Thumbnails

The thumbnail command-line option is the same as resize but ignores any image profiles that are stored in the original image. This is because these image profiles are not of much interest to thumbnail images. (Chapter 3 discusses image profiles further.) This is an example of using the thumbnail command:

```
convert -thumbnail input.jpg output.jpg
```

Cropping an Image

Another way to reduce the size of an image is by *cropping* it. Cropping is where you take a subsection of an image and remove everything surrounding that portion of the image. For example, let's say you want to change the photo of a tree to include just the top of the tree, as shown in Figure 2-10.

Figure 2-10. *The top part of the tree*

crop

To achieve this with ImageMagick, you need to specify the intended width and height of the new image and the top-left corner of that new image within the original image. For example, the image in Figure 2-10 is 1,104×372 pixels. The top-left corner of this image is at 58 pixels in and 100 pixels down. The ImageMagick command line is therefore as follows:

```
convert -crop 1104x372+58+100 input.jpg output.jpg
```

You can also specify a bottom-right corner instead, in which case you use a minus sign instead of a plus sign in the command line. You can also use gravity options with this command (discussed more in Chapter 7).

Chopping an Image

A similar concept to cropping is *chopping*. Chopping is when you remove columns and rows from the image. For example:

```
convert -chop 100x100+200+200 input.jpg output.jpg
```

Confusingly, the first two numbers here are the size of the portion of the image to remove, and the second two numbers are the location of the column and row to remove. The previous command line will give you the image shown in Figure 2-11.

Figure 2-11. *The tree with a vertical and horizontal slice removed*

Making an Image Smaller Without Specifying Dimensions

ImageMagick also allows you to make images smaller without specifying the dimensions for the new image. You can do this in two ways: trimming the image and shaving the image.

Trimming an Image

The trim command-line option is interestingly different from the operations you've seen before this. It works by removing any edge pixels that are the same color as the corner pixels. For example, if you have a picture with a solid color border such as in Figure 2-12, then trim can remove that border for you. (To see how to create borders with ImageMagick, refer to Chapter 7.)

Figure 2-12. *Another tree with a border*

If you run the following command:

```
convert -trim input.jpg output.jpg
```

then you end up with the image shown in Figure 2-13.

Figure 2-13. *The tree with most of the border removed*

You'll note that not all of the excessive border was removed. This is because the border color varies slightly as the border gets closer to the image because of the way the border command in ImageMagick works. To remove all of the border, you need to tell the trim command to be a little more forgiving in the definition of the color to remove. You can do this with the fuzz command-line option, as follows:

```
convert -fuzz 20% -trim input.jpg output.jpg
```

This gives you nearly the original image back again, as shown in Figure 2-14.

Figure 2-14. *The tree with almost all the border removed*

Shaving an Image

If you want to perform an operation such as trim but you know exactly how much of the image you want to remove, then you can use the shave command-line option instead. The shave option takes exactly amount you want to remove from the horizontal edges and vertical edges, which gives you a lot more control. For example, you know that the border in the previous example is exactly 20 pixels on each side, so you use the following command line, which will remove the border exactly:

```
convert -shave 20x20 input.jpg output.jpg
```

Understanding Geometries

Many of the previous commands take an argument that describes the size of the output image or where to start an operation (such as cropping). This command string has a generic format. The string can consist of the following components:

- `<width>x<height>`: Generally this specifies the width and height of the output image, although in some cases it is the width and height of the component to operate on (such as with the `chop` command). You can modify this width and height with these options:

  - `>`: The greater-than sign causes the width and height arguments to be used only if the current width and height are greater than that specified.

  - `<`: The less-than sign is the inverse. It causes the width and height arguments to be used only if the current width and height are less than that specified.

  - `!`: The exclamation mark inverts the logic applied by the greater-than and less-than signs.

- `%`: Instead of specifying an absolute width and height, you can also specify a percentage of the current width and height.

- `@`: The at sign specifies the maximum area of the image. The current width and height will be scaled to the maximum values available within that area while maintaining the current aspect ratio.

- `+x+y`: This option specifies the insert from the top left at which the operation will start. An example is the `crop` command previously described in this chapter.

- `-x-y`: This option specifies the same information as the previous `+x+y` option, except from the bottom right.

- `+x-y` and `-x+y`: The same as the two previous options but from the other corners.

This command-line syntax is primarily used by the `geometry` command-line option, which acts like the `resize` command. Other ImageMagick commands also use the syntax.

Making an Image Larger

What if you wanted to make an image larger instead of smaller? Although you can use all the previous resizing options in the other direction to make the image larger, it is important to remember with raster images that you don't get extra pixels for free. The pixels are created by having ImageMagick guess what should have been in the image if it had originally been made at that larger size, and by definition that guess is often not a good one.

For example, let's take the image used in earlier examples that I used to demonstrate pixels with, as shown in Figure 2-15.

Figure 2-15. *A simple input image*

If you assume that this image is small and that you want to make it four times bigger, then Figure 2-16 shows what happens.

Figure 2-16. *The simple input image once it has been made larger*

You can see that the image has become quite blocky because of the pixel-guessing process.

In general, making raster images larger is hard, and the output often won't look good at the end. You're much better off keeping an original copy of the image at as high a resolution as possible, because getting back that information is impossible once it has been thrown away by resizing an image to a smaller size.

Processing Many Images at Once

You can easily apply all the commands presented in this chapter, and many of the other commands presented in other chapters in this book, to image files using ImageMagick's `mogrify` command. The main difference between `mogrify` and `convert` is that `mogrify` natively works on many images at a time. Because these images are all specified on the command line, `mogrify` doesn't know the name of the output file like the `convert` command does. The images are therefore overwritten with the transformed images.

For example, to transform an entire directory of JPEG images into thumbnails, use the following command line:

```
mogrify -thumbnail 10% *.jpg
```

Remember that this command overwrites all the JPEG images in the directory, so you probably want to back up the images before running this command. The only exception to this overwrite behavior is if you tell `mogrify` to change the file format of the image as well. For example, you could convert all these JPEG images to PNG thumbnails, which will leave the original JPEG images untouched:

```
mogrify -format  png -thumbnail 10% *.jpg
```

Conclusion

In this chapter, I discussed some the basic image manipulations that you can perform with ImageMagick. All these transformations involve changing the size of images—be that making them larger or smaller. I also talked about the differences between raster and vector images and about some of the issues associated with resizing raster images.

In the next chapter, you'll look at how to change the file format used to store an image, how to change the parameters used by the compression algorithm used for a given image, and how to change other metadata associated with the image. In later chapters, I'll discuss other interesting topics such as the artistic transformations that you can apply to images, how to create images from scratch with ImageMagick drawing commands, and how to handle animations.

CHAPTER 3

■■■

Introducing Compression and Other Metadata

In this chapter, I'll cover how to change the compression used to encode an image file, image formats that can contain more than one image, animations (which are really a special case of the multi-image formats), and other metadata that can be associated with images. Whilst the chapter might sound dry, it will cover a lot of interesting, powerful techniques.

Compressing Images

One of the most common tasks performed with ImageMagick is to change the file format and therefore the compression algorithm used to encode an image file. Imagine for a second that someone has just e-mailed a TIFF file for you to post online, and you want to make the file smaller and better supported by most browsers so you decide to convert it to a JPEG file. How do you perform that conversion? You use ImageMagick's convert command, of course. Here's an example:

```
convert input.png output.jpg
```

This will perform the conversion for you. How you decide what file format to use can be a complex proposition, however, and this chapter will attempt to guide you through the various options that are available.

Lossy Compression vs. Lossless Compression

Compression algorithms can be lossy or lossless. A *lossless* compression algorithm guarantees that when the image is decompressed, all the data that you started with is still available. A *lossy* compression algorithm, on the other hand, will give you an approximation of the original image back when it's decompressed. In return, you have a smaller compressed file than you would with a lossless compression algorithm.

The other factor to take into account is that the loss of lossy compression algorithms accumulates. Let's say you take an image and compress it. Then in a separate operation you need to compress it again; for example, you rotate the image. Each time you recompress the image, you come up with a new approximation of the input image, and the input image for the second round of compression is the output image from the first round. This can result in quite noticeable image artifacts occurring over time.

In general, lossy compression algorithms are good for high-resolution photographs and movies, whilst lossless compression algorithms are good for low-resolution images and images containing a lot of text or line art. I'll now show some examples to demonstrate this. Figure 3-1 shows a photo of Australia's Uluru, which has been compressed with a JPEG quality of 50 percent.

Figure 3-1. *A photo compressed with a JPEG quality of 50 percent*

■**Note** You'll find out more about JPEG quality and what it actually means a little later in this section. For now, just bear in mind that a quality of 50 percent is a quite poor quality image; image quality has been sacrificed for small image size.

Figure 3-2 shows an image of some text that I'll use to demonstrate the accumulating loss.

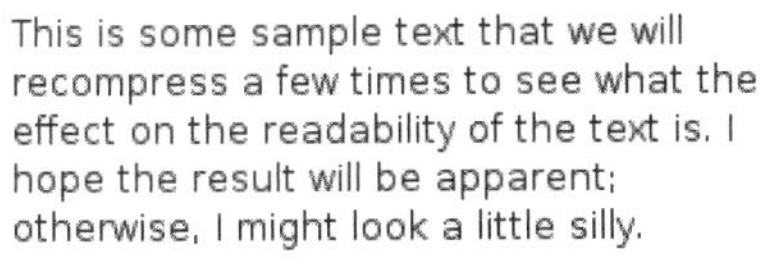

This is some sample text that we will
recompress a few times to see what the
effect on the readability of the text is. I
hope the result will be apparent;
otherwise, I might look a little silly.

Figure 3-2. *Some text before JPEG compression*

Don't focus too much on the text in the image; I'll use it for another example in a second. You can see from this example that the photo is actually of a usable quality (although not perfect). If you compress this image with a JPEG quality of 50 percent, as shown in Figure 3-3, then you can see that the text is already after only one compression starting to have a shadow around it from relatively low-quality compression.

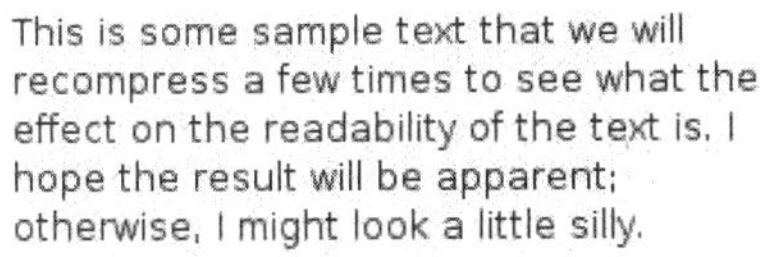

This is some sample text that we will
recompress a few times to see what the
effect on the readability of the text is. I
hope the result will be apparent;
otherwise, I might look a little silly.

Figure 3-3. *Some text compressed with a JPEG quality of 50 percent*

If you were to compress this image more than once, then the quality loss would start to accumulate. Figure 3-4 shows the image after it has been compressed ten times.

This is some sample text that we will
recompress a few times to see what the
effect on the readability of the text is. I
hope the result will be apparent;
otherwise, I might look a little silly.

Figure 3-4. *Some text after ten sets of JPEG compression loss*

You can see the gray shadow around the text getting worse, and the text is therefore getting harder to read. Now I'll present the pictures compressed with a lossless compression algorithm, such as PNG. Figure 3-5 shows the Uluru photo, and Figure 3-6 shows the text.

Figure 3-5. *A picture compressed with the lossless PNG compression*

This is some sample text that we will
recompress a few times to see what the
effect on the readability of the text is. I
hope the result will be apparent;
otherwise, I might look a little silly.

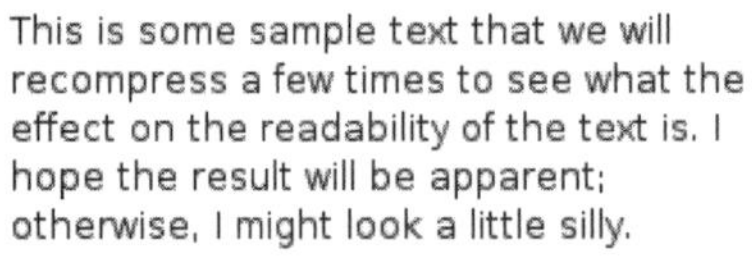

Figure 3-6. *Some text compressed with the lossless PNG compression*

So, given that the image quality is so much higher with a lossless compression algorithm such as PNG, why would you use something lossy such as JPEG compression? The simple answer is file size. The higher the JPEG lossiness, the smaller the file size you have to store on disk, and this can be handy in many situations, such as when you want to e-mail a picture to someone or serve many pictures from a Web site. Figure 3-7 compares the file sizes for a lossy compression algorithm against no compression and against PNG compression.

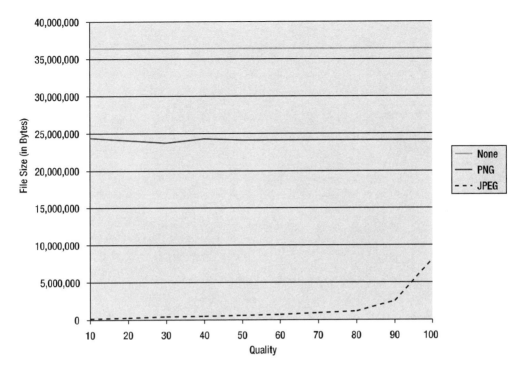

Figure 3-7. *Comparative file size for various JPEG compression qualities*

You can see in this graph that no compression is by far the largest option, and PNG offers a middle ground. Depending on the JPEG quality used, you can see that the image size will vary but is always smaller than both the uncompressed option and the PNG compression option. The uncompressed option is a straight line because there is no concept of quality.

For reference, the picture used for this graph is the 4,256×2,848 photo shown in Figure 3-8.

Figure 3-8. *The original picture used for Figure 3-7*

Finally, it's important to remember that an image quality loss is associated with using lower JPEG compression qualities. To give you a visual example of this, the image in Figure 3-9 starts at the left with a JPEG quality of 1 percent and moves across the image using increasing quality until the right side, which was compressed with 100 percent quality. The original concept for this image came from the Wikipedia page on JPEG compression (http://en.wikipedia.org/wiki/JPEG), which has an excellent discussion on the topic.

Figure 3-9. *A photo compressed with a variety of JPEG compression qualities. The highest quality is on the right, and the lowest is on the left.*

Which Format Is Right for You?

Which format is the right choice for your problem will depend on how you intend to use the image. The following sections present a decision flowchart to help you decide what image format is right for your given situation.

Archival Images

If faithful archival of the image is important, then use a lossless compression algorithm to avoid having image data discarded as part of the compression process. Once this image data has been discarded, it's impossible to recover.

Black-and-White Images

Black-and-white images are much smaller than their full-color equivalents, and the size penalty on disk of a losslessly compressed image is much smaller. It's therefore often much more acceptable to store these images using a lossless compression algorithm. Also, specialized compression algorithms work best with black-and-white images, which you should consider using. The main contenders here are CCITT Group 3 Fax and CCITT Group 4 Fax, which, as their names suggest, were developed for transmitting fax images. The compression algorithms work well with black-and-white image data but do not work for color images.

Images Containing Large Amounts of Text

If the image in question contains text, or is mostly relevant because of the text stored within it, then strongly consider using a lossless compression format. The blur associated with the approximations developed by a lossy compression format will make the image much harder to read later.

Images Containing Detailed Line Art

For similar reasons to the images containing text, if the clarity of line art is important to your use of the images, then use a lossless compression format so that the line art doesn't become blurred.

You Need a Small File

If you intend to e-mail the image or serve it many times from a Web site, then a small file might be the best solution. In that case, you should use a lossy compression format. For example, at Christmas 2003 my personal Web site got "Slashdotted" and served 39 gigabytes in a 24-hour period. The page that was Slashdotted contained a number of PNG images, which take 4.2 megabytes in total. This meant that for every hit on that one page, I had to serve 4.2 megabytes of pictures as well. If these images had been encoded with JPEG at a quality of 75 percent, then they would have been only 484 kilobytes. This would have meant I could have reduced the data served by about 38 gigabytes. You live, and you learn.

Photographic Images

Finally, photos have special compression needs because they're often so large. Many of the digital cameras on the market now, for instance, shoot at more than 5 megapixels, which makes for very large uncompressed images. Lossy compression algorithms such as JPEG work well with these images because they're such a high resolution that you don't notice the image quality loss associated with the lossy compression unless the images are blown up really large or are manipulated too many times.

The other thing to bear in mind is that most digital cameras are already shooting in JPEG by default, so your images probably start in this format if they're photos. Some nicer cameras will also shoot in an uncompressed format called RAW, which leaves your options open.

Introducing Common File Formats

So far I've discussed the two styles of compression system available for images—lossy compression and lossless compression. Later in the chapter, I'll talk about some actual example images and how much they're compressed with these different styles, but before that I'll introduce common examples of each compression style and explain what each style is commonly used for. You can find more information on all the image formats that ImageMagick supports at http://www.imagemagick.org/script/formats.php if you need more information than is presented here.

By far the most common lossy compression algorithm in use today is a file format called JPEG. JPEG stands for the Joint Photographic Experts Group, which formed in 1985. The output of that working group was the compression algorithm now known as JPEG. JPEG itself is actually a bit stream format, and the first file format to use JPEG was the JPEG File Interchange Format (JFIF), which is now commonly known as JPEG and is what most digital cameras produce. JPEG is also being used for image storage; for example, the container format TIFF optionally stores JPEG bit streams as well. JPEG is well supported by many applications, including viewers, editors, and Web browsers.

On the other hand, many lossless compression algorithms are available. The Portable Network Graphics (PNG) file format and the Tagged Image File Format (TIFF) are common examples, although TIFF can use the lossy JPEG compression as well. Less common examples are the Graphics Interchange Format (GIF) and the Microsoft Windows bitmap (BMP) format.

PNG is a good choice for storing images in a lossless manner because it's well supported by a large selection of tools, including viewers and editors. Modern browsers (those with a version number greater than 3) support PNG images as well.

The TIFF container format is interesting because it allows for the use of various compression algorithms, which is unusual for an image format. This makes the format flexible and means that many high-end editing applications use TIFF. Because TIFF is such a large and flexible image format, many image viewers and editors have trouble opening all possible TIFF files. However, certain tools can convert your TIFF images into the supported subset for a given application. Web browsers don't support TIFF without using plug-ins, so it's a bad choice for online purposes.

Introducing LZW Compression

LZW compression is the compression scheme used in the GIF file format. Unisys, as the owner of U.S. Patent 4,558,302, realized that the GIF file format uses LZW compression in 1994, at which time GIF had been an accepted image format for many years. As a result, Unisys started requiring a patent license of Web sites using GIF images. This resulted in a campaign to remove GIF support from many open-source image-processing applications, including ImageMagick. Many Web sites also stopped using GIF at this time.

Since this time, the LZW patent has expired, and it's now possible to add support for LZW and therefore GIF to ImageMagick at compile time. Many open source developers are still hesitant to support LZW, however, so you need to enable support explicitly. If you installed a binary version of ImageMagick as described in Chapter 1, you may have such support enabled.

If LZW support isn't enabled and you ask ImageMagick to perform an operation that would result in an LZW compressed image being created, then a form of LZW that isn't covered by the patent will be used. This form results in no compression occurring, which means you might create GIF files that are bigger than you expect.

Comparing File Sizes

You can find an exhaustive list of the image formats supported by ImageMagick at `http://www.imagemagick.org/script/formats.php`. I'll now show some examples of the more common image compression formats and how the different compression schemes they implement can affect file size. I'll cover color image formats first. Table 3-1 compares the sizes of the image shown in Figure 3-10 when compressed with a variety of formats.

Table 3-1. *Comparative Sizes for an Image Compressed with Various Options*

Compression	Quality	File Size (Bytes)
JPEG	10%	111,202
	20%	147,575
	30%	187,105
	40%	225,945
	50%	271,854
	60%	329,787
	70%	431,488
	80%	631,369
	90%	1,149,447
	100%	3,883,520
BMP		23,887,926
BMP2		23,887,898
BMP3		23,887,926
GIF		4,806,309
PICT		3,692,672
PNG	10%	15,835,876
	20%	15,673,758
	30%	15,468,303
	40%	15,884,182
	50%	15,814,211
	60%	15,783,707
	70%	15,777,354
	80%	15,774,804
	90%	15,774,774
	100%	15,774,774
RAW		2,686,535
TIFF with LZW		23,105,716
TIFF with Packbits		23,886,580
TIFF with zip		17,225,512
No compression		23,906,618

Figure 3-10. *The photo used for Table 3-1*

Manipulating Compression Options with ImageMagick

After all this talk of which compression algorithm you should use for different tasks, I'll spend some time discussing how to manipulate compression with ImageMagick. The most obvious example of what you might want to do is convert between compression formats. For example, you can convert a JPEG file to a PNG file as follows:

```
convert input.jpg output.png
```

This will work for any format that uses only one compression algorithm, such as PNG or JPEG. It will work with formats that can use more than one compression algorithm, such as TIFF, by using the default compression algorithm.

Specifying a Compression

If you need to specify the compression algorithm for such a format, then use the compress option:

```
convert -compress zip input.jpg output.tif
```

This example produces a TIFF image that has been compressed with zip compression (also known as *deflate* compression). These are the possible compression options to use with the compress command:

- None

- Bzip

- Fax (CCITT Group 3 fax compression)

- Group4 (CCITT Group 4 fax compression)

- JPEG

- JPEG2000

- Lossless (lossless JPEG)

- LZW

- RLE (run-length encoding)

- Zip (also known as *deflate* compression)

For a complete list the image formats supported by ImageMagick that can use the compress option, see the ImageMagick Web site at http://www.imagemagick.org/script/formats.php.

Specifying a Quality

Several of the file formats supported by ImageMagick have tunable compression where the quality of the compression can be changed. The interpretation of the quality argument does vary with format, however. Earlier in the chapter I discussed JPEG quality, and at the time I used the input image shown in Figure 3-11.

Figure 3-11. *The original picture*

As mentioned earlier, I then produced an image split into vertical columns of different qualities, as inspired by an example on Wikipedia, as shown in Figure 3-12.

Figure 3-12. *A photo compressed with a variety of JPEG compression qualities. The highest quality is on the right, and the lowest is on the left.*

Interestingly, if I repeat this experiment using PNG compression, I get the output shown in Figure 3-13.

Figure 3-13. *A photo compressed with a variety of PNG compression qualities. The highest quality is on the right, and the lowest is on the left.*

You can see here that there is no noticeable decrease in the quality of the image when it's decompressed. This is because the PNG compressor uses the `quality` argument as a way of determining how much computational effort to expend on finding the smallest possible compressed version, as opposed to how much image data to throw away. Therefore, you'll always get the same quality image when you decompress, but the time taken to compress the image will change.

You specify a quality with the `quality` command-line option. For example, to produce a JPEG image that is pretty lossy but in return quite small, you can use the following command line:

```
convert -quality 10% input.jpg output.jpg
```

This will produce the lower-quality file for you.

Creating Interlaced Images

Interlacing allows images to be displayed progressively as they're downloaded. You might even have noticed this behavior on Web pages, which is the most common place it's used. This means users on lower-bandwidth connections can get a sense of the image contents before the image has been fully downloaded. ImageMagick sets the interlacing order for formats that support it using the `interlace` command-line option.

Use the `line` or `plane` values to create a progressive image, as follows:

```
convert -interlace line input.jpg output.jpg
```

Passing Other Parameters to Coders and Decoders

ImageMagick calls the software that compresses images for it *coders* and the software that decompresses an image a *decoder*. Normally the encoding and decoding will be implemented by the same package, which is often a library that ImageMagick used during the compilation process described in Chapter 1.

You might want to pass other information to the coder or decoder. ImageMagick lets you do this with the `define` command-line argument. It takes a key and a value for the coder or decoder to use. For example, the JPEG 2000 coder can take a compression factor that affects the size and quality of the output image. You specify it like this:

```
convert input.jpg -define "jp2:rate=0.5" output.jp2
```

If you need to remove a definition that is defined, then you can use the `+define` command-line argument with a plus sign at the start to remove the definition:

```
convert +define "jp2:rate" input.jpg output.jpg
```

To remove all definitions, use the following command line:

```
convert input.jpg +define "*" output.ps
```

Introducing the JPEG and MPEG Sampling Factor

Both JPEG and MPEG (which stands for Moving Picture Experts Group, the group that defined the MPEG video format) images are stored in the YUV color space. With RGB images, the red, green, and blue samples are generally stored in an interlaced manner (although this isn't always the case). YUV color space has three separate sets of image information; the *Y* stands for luminance, and the *U* and *V* are chrominance information. As an example, I recently had to convert some YUV image data from a Web camera into RGB. During that process I ended up generating this test image to help me tell whether my conversion worked, as shown in Figure 3-14.

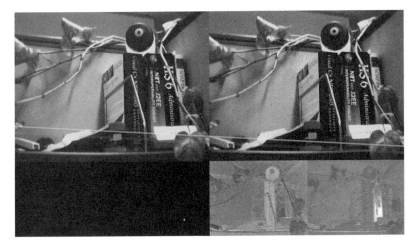

Figure 3-14. *An RGB image on the left and a YUV image on the right*

The image on the left is the RGB version, and the three images on the right form the YUV components. You can see here that the Y information (the luminance) is simply a black-and-white version on the image, whereas the U and V components are color information and therefore a little more complicated.

YUV images can have different sizes for the Y component and the U and V components. You can see this in Figure 3-14, where the Y component is twice the size horizontally and vertically of the U and V components. This is because the YUV example here is actually a YUV 4:2:2 image. This process of having smaller images for the U and V components is called *chroma subsampling*.

ImageMagick allows you to specify what YUV chroma subsampling you'd like by using the sampling-factor command-line option, which lets you specify a horizontal sampling factor and a vertical sampling factor. For example, to convert a PNG into YUV 4:2:2, you'd use this command line:

```
convert -sampling-factor 2x1 input.png output.jpg
```

For an excellent coverage of JPEG, refer to http://en.wikipedia.org/wiki/JPEG. For more information about YUV, check out the Wikipedia page at http://en.wikipedia.org/wiki/YUV.

Introducing Image Metadata

Metadata is data about data. In the imaging world, this is generally information about the image, which is stored in the image file as well. Examples of commonly used image metadata include the time the picture was created, the name of the author, and so forth. Here's an example of the metadata stored by one of my digital cameras when I take a photo:

```
Image: input.jpg
  Format: JPEG (Joint Photographic Experts Group JFIF format)
  Geometry: 3456x2304
  Class: DirectClass
  Colorspace: RGB
  Type: TrueColor
  Depth: 8 bits
  Endianess: Undefined
  Channel depth:
    Red: 8-bits
    Green: 8-bits
    Blue: 8-bits
  Channel statistics:
    Red:
      Min: 0
      Max: 255
      Mean: 63.6148
      Standard deviation: 46.6134
    Green:
      Min: 0
      Max: 254
```

```
  Mean: 37.6559
    Standard deviation: 35.9952
  Blue:
    Min: 0
    Max: 255
    Mean: 24.2289
    Standard deviation: 35.2562
Colors: 70398
Rendering-intent: Undefined
Resolution: 72x72
Units: Undefined
Filesize: 2.5mb
Interlace: None
Background Color: grey100
Border Color: #DFDFDF
Matte Color: grey74
Dispose: Undefined
Iterations: 0
Compression: JPEG
Orientation: Undefined
JPEG-Quality: 98
JPEG-Colorspace: 2
JPEG-Sampling-factors: 2x1,1x1,1x1
signature: 64c4132c69f7fcc2398ff722f6920e93f7324f6672d489002b53f1538c50c946
Profile-exif: 15108 bytes
  Make: Canon.
  Model: Canon EOS 350D DIGITAL.
  Orientation: 8
  X Resolution: 72/1
  Y Resolution: 72/1
  Resolution Unit: 2
  Date Time: 2005:06:23 09:22:51.
  Y Cb Cr Positioning: 2
  Exif Offset: 196
  Exposure Time: 1/60
  F Number: 56/10
  Exposure Program: 2
  ISO Speed Ratings: 400
  Exif Version: 0221
  Date Time Original: 2005:06:23 09:22:51.
  Date Time Digitized: 2005:06:23 09:22:51.
  Components Configuration: ....
  Shutter Speed Value: 387114/65536
  Aperture Value: 325770/65536
  Exposure Bias Value: 0/2
  Metering Mode: 5
  Flash: 89
```

```
            Focal Length: 55/1
            Flash Pix Version: 0100
            Color Space: 1
            Exif Image Width: 3456
            Exif Image Length: 2304
            Interoperability Offset: 9230
            unknown: R98.
            unknown: 0100
            Focal PlaneX Resolution: 3456000/874
            Focal PlaneY Resolution: 2304000/582
            Focal Plane Resolution Unit: 2
            unknown: 0
            unknown: 0
            unknown: 0
            unknown: 0
      Tainted: False
      User Time: 1.580u
      Elapsed Time: 0:02
```

You can see that a lot of information is stored within the JPEG file. I extracted this list of information with the following ImageMagick command:

```
identify -verbose input.jpg
```

This is the first time I've mentioned the identify command in this book. You can find more complete coverage of the identify command in Chapter 4. Here I've asked the identify command to list all the metadata that it can about the input file.

■Note Some of the metadata from the previous dump isn't actually stored in the image file but is generated by the identify command when needed. It is still, however, metadata.

A lot of the information stored here is really quite useful. For example, the orientation information is used by my Web interface for cataloging pictures from my camera so that I don't need to manually decide which images should be rotated; you'll see more of this Web interface in Chapter 8. The date and time information is useful for searching. The focal length and ISO speed, and so forth, are useful for tracking my journey through learning how to use an SLR camera. Fundamentally, having more information is always better than having less when it comes to images. You can always ignore the information that isn't important.

Another advantage of metadata in image formats that support it is that the information is always with the image. You'll have no need to move around extra files that contain this useful information, because it's embedded in the image file. This is something you should be aware of, though, because there might be privacy implications in handing out some of this information, depending on your needs.

Most of this metadata survives image transformations with ImageMagick, as long as the new image format also supports those metadata fields. For example, if I resize the image that

I extracted this metadata from, then I still get the same metadata from the smaller image. The only exceptions are the metadata that relates to the size of the image and some additional metadata that ImageMagick inserts in the file to indicate that the image has been transformed.

To strip the metadata from an image to avoid these privacy concerns, add the strip command-line argument to the convert command, like so:

```
convert -strip input.jpg output.jpg
```

The metadata for the output file is now as follows:

```
output.jpg JPEG 3456x2304 DirectClass 2.5mb 0.740u 0:01
Image: output.jpg
  Format: JPEG (Joint Photographic Experts Group JFIF format)
  Geometry: 3456x2304
  Class: DirectClass
  Type: TrueColor
  Endianess: Undefined
  Colorspace: RGB
  Channel depth:
    Red: 8-bits
    Green: 8-bits
    Blue: 8-bits
  Channel statistics:
    Red:
      Min: 0 (0)
      Max: 255 (1)
      Mean: 63.6277 (0.24952)
      Standard deviation: 46.6054 (0.182766)
    Green:
      Min: 0 (0)
      Max: 254 (0.996078)
      Mean: 37.6472 (0.147636)
      Standard deviation: 35.9972 (0.141166)
    Blue:
      Min: 0 (0)
      Max: 255 (1)
      Mean: 24.2631 (0.0951495)
      Standard deviation: 35.241 (0.1382)
  Colors: 69340
  Rendering-intent: Undefined
  Resolution: 72x72
  Units: PixelsPerInch
  Filesize: 2.5mb
  Interlace: None
  Background Color: white
  Border Color: #DFDFDF
  Matte Color: grey74
  Dispose: Undefined
```

```
Iterations: 0
Compression: JPEG
Quality: 98
Orientation: Undefined
JPEG-Colorspace: 2
JPEG-Sampling-factors: 2x1,1x1,1x1
Signature: 9edbbbdfe4d51f09da2c9499ce1799dc5a1a17bae53b3f6189130db1b755291e
Tainted: False
Version: ImageMagick 6.2.3 06/09/05 Q16 http://www.imagemagick.org
```

You can see that this offers a lot less information, which is the desired result.

What if you wanted to change some of the attributes of the metadata stored within the file? A simple example is wanting to add or change a comment associated with the image file. You do this with the comment command-line option to the convert command. For example, add a comment to a JPEG file like so:

```
convert -comment "Mary had a little lamb" input.jpg output.jpg
```

Remember that you can also use the mogrify command to perform this operation in place, like so:

```
mogrify -comment "Mary had a little lamb" input.jpg
```

Here the input image is changed without specifying an output filename—the input file is overwritten. You can use a number of format characters to expand this to useful information (see Table 3-2).

Table 3-2. *Format Characters for the* comment *Command*

Format String	Expands To
%b	File size
%c	Comment
%d	Directory
%e	Filename extension
%f	Filename
%h	Height
%i	Input filename
%k	Number of unique colors
%l	Label
%m	Magick
%n	Number of scenes
%o	Output filename
%p	Page number
%q	Quantum depth
%r	Image class and color space
%s	Scene number

Format String	Expands To
%t	Top of filename
%u	Unique temporary filename
%w	Width
%x	x resolution
%y	y resolution
%@	Bounding box
%#	Signature
\n	New line
\r	Carriage return

Some of these format strings might seem a little odd. This is because other commands use these format strings as well. I'll discuss some other uses for these format strings in a moment. To embed a comment into the image metadata that contains the file size, for instance, use the following command line:

```
mogrify -comment "The size of the file is %b bytes" input.jpg
```

The final use for these format strings is to place information about the image into the image itself so that it's visible in the viewer as part of the image. I'll discuss this more in Chapter 7. You'll find more coverage of the mogrify command in Chapter 4.

Similarly, for image formats that support labels, you can label an image with a descriptive string. The string takes the same format as the comment. Here's an example:

```
convert -label "This is an image" input.jpg output.jpg
```

Additionally, if the first character of the comment or label is an at sign, then the remainder of the argument is taken as the filename from which to get the comment or label.

Altering How Pixels Are Stored

Not all the attributes shown in the previous identify command are strictly metadata. For example, the number of colors in the image and color space refers to the encoding of the actual image data in the file and how to decode it for display, rather than optional data about the image as metadata normally is. It's possible to change the values of these attributes, however. For example, if you wanted to reduce the number of colors used by an image, then you'd use the colors command-line option. People usually want to perform this sort of operation to reduce the size of files or to ensure that the image displays correctly on hardware that supports only a small number of concurrent colors. By reducing the number of colors that the image can use, storing individual pixels takes less space because a smaller number of possible values needs to be represented. To reduce the picture whose metadata I've shown previously from 24 bits per pixel (16,777,216 individual colors), which is the format the camera shoots in, to 256 colors, I use the following command:

```
convert -colors 256 input.tif output.tif
```

You can obtain many more details by examining the colors command-line option in Chapter 6, which includes example images.

Another example of an image attribute that isn't strictly metadata is the number of channels in the image. The TIFF terminology for channels is perhaps a little easier to understand, so I'll use that as an explanation and then show you how that correlates to channels.

With TIFF images, you can specify two numbers that are important to the way the bitmap information in the image file is stored. Before I discuss them, though, I should mention what a *sample* is. You can imagine that images from cameras and scanners involve hardware that looks at something in the real world and takes a number of readings to determine what color the different pixels in the image should be to represent the real thing in the image. Those readings are the samples.

The first attribute is the number of bits per sample, which specifies the range of possible values for a given sample. For example, if you specify eight bits per sample, then the possible range of values for the sample is 0 through to 255.

The second attribute is the number of samples per pixel. RGB images have three samples—the red one, the blue one, and the green one. If the image has a transparency sample (an alpha channel), then there are four. If the image uses a palette, then the number of samples is one, as all the color information actually comes from an entry in a lookup table (the palette) into which the sample points.

In ImageMagick parlance, these samples are called *channels*, which is the terminology I'll use for the rest of this book.

You can also change the color space that an image uses to represent the pixels in the image. A *color space* is the representation format for pixels. For example, the RGB color space uses a red, green, and blue value to represent a pixel, whereas the YUV color space, which is used in PAL television signals, uses luminance and chrominance information to achieve the same end. This is from the ImageMagick documentation:

> Color reduction, by default, takes place in the RGB color space. Empirical evidence suggests that distances in color spaces such as YUV or YIQ correspond to perceptual color differences more closely than do distances in RGB space. These color spaces may give better results when color reducing an image.

You might therefore want to select a different color space when reducing the number of colors in your image so as to produce a better-looking outcome. You can do this with the following command-line option:

```
convert -colors numberofcolors -colorspace space input.jpg output.jpg
```

where space is one of the following: CMYK, GRAY, HSL, HWB, OHTA, Rec601Luma, Rec709Luma, RGB, Transparent, XYZ, YCbCr, YIQ, YPbPr, or YUV. Selecting color spaces is a specialist field outside the scope of this book, so you're best off looking into this field more before spending too much effort on manipulating color spaces. A good place to start is the Color Space FAQ at http://www.faqs.org/faqs/graphics/colorspace-faq/.

While you're manipulating the storage of the pixels within the image, you might want to specify the maximum pixel depth. You can do this with the depth command-line option, although it should be noted that the only possible values for the depth are 8 and 16:

```
convert -depth 8 input.jpg output.jpg
```

Another attribute of the image that affects the storage of the image data is the *endianness* of the image. Endianness refers to the order in which the bytes in a word are stored. The options are little endian (LSB) and big endian (MSB), and you can set these with the endian command-line option. To specify little endian, you use a command line like this:

```
convert -endian LSB input.jpg output.jpg
```

Use a plus sign instead of a minus sign at the start of the command-line option to use the default endianness for that image format.

Finally, for the pixel storage options, you can force ImageMagick to use a particular representation for the pixels in the image. The following options are available:

- Bilevel: A black-and-white image where pixels are either on or off.

- Grayscale: Pixels are able to have only one sample, which is why they're not color.

- Palette: Colors are stored elsewhere in the file, and each pixel references an entry in this table.

- PaletteMatte: A palette with an alpha (transparency) channel.

- TrueColor: A full RGB image.

- TrueColorMatte: A full RGB image with an alpha channel. Often known as RGBA.

- ColorSeparation: Colors are stored separately in the bitmap, so all the red values are stored together, then all the green, and then all the blue, for example.

- ColorSeparationMatte: Same as ColorSeparation but with an alpha channel.

- Optimize: Whatever works best with the formats you're working with and the pixel values actually used in the image.

Here's an example of forcing an image to use a palette:

```
convert -type Palette input.jpg output.jpg
```

Introducing Gamma Correction

Most monitors aren't calibrated to produce exactly the same colors as other monitors; such calibration is reserved for generally more expensive hardware. This is why when you put two monitors next to each other and display the same image, you'll often get different colors in the images displayed. You can use *gamma correction* to calibrate images so that they display properly. Gamma correction is of particular interest to the print industry, which uses it to ensure that what the artist sees on the screen is what is produced on paper. With ImageMagick, you can specify a gamma correction value with the gamma command-line option, like this:

```
convert -gamma 1.7 input.png output.jpg
```

If you need to specify a different gamma correction value for each color channel in the image, then just separate them with a comma. This example specifies values for the red, green, and blue channels in that order:

```
convert -gamma 1.7,2.3,0.7 input.png output.jpg
```

Setting Color Intent and Profiles

The International Color Consortium (ICC) has defined a set of color intents for images that ImageMagick supports:

- Perceptual: The full range of possible colors in the output device should be used. The relative spacing of colors is maintained, so if a color falls outside the range of colors possible on the device, then the space between all colors will be reduced.

- Saturation: This preserves the separation of colors.

- Relative: If a color falls outside the range of colors possible, the closest possible color is used. Other colors remain unchanged.

- Absolute: This is the same as relative, but the white point of the image is preserved.

This is a fairly technical field, so if you need more information, check out the excellent explanation on the Microsoft MSDN site at http://msdn.microsoft.com/library/default.asp?url=/library/en-us/icm/icm_0e43.asp. To have ImageMagick set the intent of the image, use the following command line:

```
mogrify -intent absolute input.jpg
```

Images can also store a color profile, which is added to an image with the profile command-line option. You can remove the profile information from the image with the +profile command-line option:

```
mogrify +profile input.jpg
```

Handling Images That Don't Specify Dimensions

ImageMagick supports several image formats that don't encode the dimensions of the image into the image file. In fact, these documents store no metadata, just the image bitmap itself. You can specify the size of the image on the command line, which ImageMagick needs in order to convert the image to other formats. To do this, just use a command line like the following:

```
convert -size widthxheight input.raw output.jpg
```

where width is the horizontal dimension and height is the vertical. The image formats for which you'll need to do this are RGB, Gray, and CMYK.

Setting Image Resolution

Another example of a piece of metadata that won't directly affect the display of the image in most cases but that is part of the image encoding is the image resolution. Some devices, such as printers, will use this for displaying the image. On-screen display will normally ignore it, however. You can specify the resolution of the image with the density command-line option:

```
convert -density widthxheight
```

where width is the horizontal resolution and height is the vertical resolution. You can specify the units for the resolution as well. The three options are as follows:

- Undefined

- PixelsPerInch

- PixelsPerCentimeter

Here's an example of setting the resolution of an image to 72 pixels per inch:

```
convert -density 72x72 -units PixelsPerInch
```

Transparency with GIF

GIF doesn't store an alpha channel in the same way as other image formats. Instead, the GIF file nominates a color that is transparent and then treats any occurrences of that color as being 100 percent transparent. You can specify this transparent color for GIF files with ImageMagick using the transparent command-line option. Here's an example of setting blue to transparent in a GIF file:

```
convert -transparent blue input.gif output.gif
```

This will result in any occurrences of the pure blue color being treated as 100 percent transparent when the image is displayed.

Storing Multiple Image Formats

Some image formats support storing more than one image per file. The most common examples are TIFF files and Adobe's Portable Document Format (PDF). ImageMagick can extract all the images from one of these multiple image formats, as well as create these formats. For example, this extracts all the pages from a PDF document into separate PNG files:

```
convert input.pdf output-%d.png
```

This will produce a series of files named output-0.png, output-1.png, and so forth. To exert more control over the name of the output files, you can use standard printf schematics to control the format of the number inserted. The most interesting option available is to pad the number with leading zeros. To do this, use a format string like this:

```
%03d
```

The leading zero says to pad the number with leading zeros. The 3 says to create a three-digit number. You'll end up with numbers of the following form:

```
000
001
002
003
004
```

This means that the output files will sort properly in Windows Explorer or in a command-line directory listing command such as ls or dir. If you don't specify %d, then ImageMagick will append a unique number to the end of the output filename. For example, the following command:

```
convert input.pdf output.png
```

will produce these output files:

```
output.png.0
output.png.1
```

This is a lot less useful, because many applications assume that the file extension portion (the part after the last period) indicates the format of the file.

Adding, Removing, and Swapping Images

ImageMagick can add and remove images from these multiple image formats with ease. To add another image into the file, use the `insert` command-line option:

```
convert -insert 4 newimage.gif input.gif output.gif
```

This command will insert a new frame from the file `newimage.gif` as the fourth image of the animation stored in `input.gif` and save the new animation to `output.gif`. The images after the fourth image are shifted down to make room. To delete frames from an animation, use the `delete` command-line option with a list of the images to delete. For example, to delete every second frame from a GIF animation with seven frames, you'd use the following command line:

```
convert -delete 2,4,6 input.gif output.gif
```

This will give the appearance that the animation is happening faster, as well as making the file size smaller. You can also use this command-line option on other multiple image formats, such as TIFF files.

You can even swap two images:

```
convert -swap 3,4 input.gif, output.gif
```

This will swap the third and fourth frames in the animation. Although I've used an animation as an example here, these command-line options will work just as well on nonanimated formats such as PDF and TIFF.

Creating Multiple Image Files

You can create a multi-image file from scratch by specifying a list of files to turn into the multi-image file. It's as simple as this:

```
convert image1.jpg image2.jpg image3.jpg output.pdf
```

This will produce a PDF document that has each of these input images as a page in the document.

Decrypting Encrypted PDFs

Adobe's PDF format supports the encryption of the content of the document. This affects ImageMagick's ability to extract images from PDF documents that have this encryption enabled. To decrypt the document and extract the images, use the `authenticate` command-line option, as shown here:

```
convert -authenticate password input.pdf output%d.png
```

This will use the password specified as needed to extract the images from the PDF file into the PNG files specified.

Manipulating Animated Images

Some of the formats supported by ImageMagick that can contain multiple images are animations. Examples of this include GIF animations, MPEG movies, and Microsoft's Audio Video Interleave (AVI) video format. ImageMagick has a number of facilities to help with handling these formats.

Changing the Frame Rate

You can change the frame rate at which an animation runs with the `delay` command-line option. Essentially, this adds a delay between the display of each frame, although this is implemented by adding extra identical frames to the animation. The argument to the `delay` command-line option is the number of hundreds of a second to delay. For example, if you wanted to take a series of JPEG files and produce an MPEG movie where each new image appears after a second, then you'd use the `delay` command and pass a value of 100:

```
convert -delay 100 frames-*.jpg output.mpg
```

Because this is implemented with packing in extra frames, you should be aware that it can have quite noticeable effects on the time it takes to generate the animation and the final file size.

Morphing Two Images

To morph two images together, use the `morph` command-line option. Morph takes as its argument a list of the frames to morph together and writes out either an animation or a set of frames. For example, the following command line will morph the two files `one.png` and `two.png` and write three frames out with the names `output-0.png`, `output-1.png`, and `output-2.png`:

```
convert -morph 1,2 one.png two.png output-%d.png
```

Creating Looping GIF Animations

In some circumstances, you don't want an animation to end once it's played; instead, you want it to return to the beginning and start again. The most common example of this is animated GIF files for Web sites, where the actual animation is often only a few frames long and the visual effect is largely achieved through this looping. You can flag a GIF animation as looping with ImageMagick by using the `loop` command-line option, where the argument is the number of times to repeat. For an endlessly looping GIF animation, use the value 0 as the argument:

```
convert -loop 0 frames-*.gif output.gif
```

Note that looping GIFs is a feature introduced in early versions of Netscape, and older software might not handle it properly. To introduce a pause in the animation before starting the animation again, use the `pause` command-line option. For example, to loop through an animation three times, with a delay of five seconds between each display of the animation, you use a command line like this:

```
convert -loop 3 -pause 5 frames-*.gif output.gif
```

Using GIF Disposal

The GIF image format allows you to specify what should be done with a frame once it has been displayed. The options are as follows:

- `Undefined`: This replaces the old frame with the new one.

- `None`: Visible pixels from the previous frame continue to be displayed.

- `Background`: The previous frame is visible through transparent pixels in the new frame.

- `Previous`: This restores to a previously undisposed frame.

For a good tutorial on GIF disposal, see `http://www.webreference.com/content/studio/disposal.html`. You can specify the GIF disposal method with the `dispose` command-line option, as follows:

```
convert -dispose background input.gif output.gif
```

Harnessing Disposal Methods

Disposal methods have two interesting side effects. You can use the `deconstruct` command-line option to use disposal to produce animations that are much smaller, as subsequent frames store only differences from the previous frame. For example, this command line:

```
convert -deconstruct input.gif output.gif
```

turns the GIF animation in this example from being 13,717 bytes to 8,854 bytes. You can also do the opposite—you can take an animation that uses disposal and force each frame to store the entire animation state, instead of relying on the last frame for some of its display, like so:

```
convert -coalesce input.gif output.gif
```

This will produce a large animation again.

Conclusion

In this chapter, you looked at how to change the compression of an image, the attributes of the compression of an image, or even the entire format of the image. You also learned how to handle multiple image formats such as TIFF and PDF, including creating them, removing single images from them, and swapping images within them. Finally, I talked about the ultimate in multiple image formats—animations.

In the next chapter, I'll cover some of the other ImageMagick command-line tools before presenting some of the more artistic transformations that ImageMagick can perform on an image.

■■■

Using Other ImageMagick Tools

Most of this book discusses the `convert` command, but several other interesting tools ship with ImageMagick. I'll introduce these tools in this chapter and show how to use them as relevant throughout this book; for example, Chapter 3 showed how to use the `mogrify` command to update the metadata in image files. ImageMagick has two classes of tools: the command-line tools and the tools with graphical user interfaces. I'll discuss these two types of tools in separate sections of this chapter.

Using the Command-Line Tools

I'll discuss the command-line tools that ship with ImageMagick in alphabetical order in the following sections so you can use this chapter as a reference guide.

compare

The `compare` command creates a graphical representation of the differences between two images, and it gives you a mathematical measurement of the difference between the two images. In this section, I'll show the effects of the command on a picture I took during a recent hot-air-balloon ride. Figure 4-1 shows the input image.

Figure 4-1. *The original image*

Chapter 5 discusses the spread command-line argument, but for now I'll show the output of the spread command and use it as example input for the compare command. Figure 4-2 shows a spread operation with an argument of 1.

Figure 4-2. *The original image, spread by a factor of 1*

The `compare` command will show you the differences between these two images graphically. If you run the following command:

```
compare original.jpg changed.jpg compared.jpg
```

then the final image in the command line will contain the differences between the first two images on the command line. For this example, the output looks like Figure 4-3.

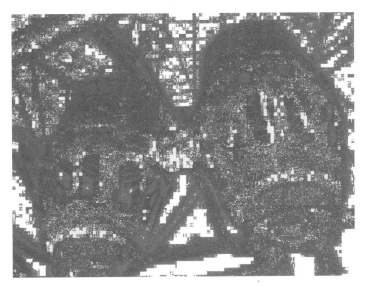

Figure 4-3. *The differences between the original image and the image that was spread by a factor of 1*

The effect of the `spread` command-line argument becomes more pronounced as the factor increases. (Again, you can find a full explanation of the `spread` command-line option in Chapter 5.) Briefly, `spread` takes a random pixel within the circle surrounding the current pixel and swaps the two. The argument to the `spread` command is the radius of that circle. Figure 4-4 shows a spread factor of 10, and Figure 4-5 shows the differences.

Figure 4-4. *The original image, spread by a factor of 10*

Figure 4-5. *The differences between the original image and the image that was spread by a factor of 10*

The `compare` command has some options as well. To compare only some channels, use the `channel` command-line argument, which lets you select on which channels the comparison occurs. (You can also use the `channel` argument with the `convert` command if you want to apply a conversion to only selected channels.) Additionally, you can compare just a portion of an image using the `extract` command-line argument to `compare`. This command-line argument takes a `geometry` argument, as discussed in Chapter 2.

Note Chapter 3 explains channels in more detail, but in summary a channel is one of the samples for a given pixel; for example, an RGB image contains a red channel, a green channel, and a blue channel.

You can also select the metric used to measure the difference between pixels with the `metric` command-line argument. Selecting a metric is a highly technical area that is out of scope for this book, so I recommend you refer to the ImageMagick documentation at `http://www.imagemagick.org/script/compare.php` for more information. If the images are large, then the comparison can take quite some time, in which case you can use the `monitor` command-line argument to show the progress of the command. For example, here's a comparison with a `monitor` command-line argument, followed by its output:

```
compare -monitor input1.png input2.png compare.png
```

```
Mogrify image: 100%
Save image: 100%
```

This progress information updates as the command runs.

composite

The `composite` command allows you to overlay one image on another. In the past, the `composite` command was the `combine` command, so if you can't find the `composite` command in your ImageMagick installation, look for `combine` instead. Many of the `convert` command-line options are also implemented by the `composite` command. In this section, I'll focus on the command-line options that are unique to the `composite` command. Specifically, as an example of how to use the `composite` command, I'll show how to annotate the photo in Figure 4-6 with some text.

Let's say you want to put the image shown in Figure 4-7 on top of the one shown in Figure 4-6.

Figure 4-6. *A picture of a golf ball on grass*

Step 1 to a good golf game:
Hit the ball with the club.

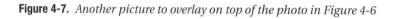

Figure 4-7. *Another picture to overlay on top of the photo in Figure 4-6*

To composite these images, be sure to name the image that will be on top first, because the second image is the one that dictates the size of the output image. This is the command line to use:

```
composite ontop.png underneath.png output.png
```

This produces the output image in Figure 4-8.

Figure 4-8. *The output image after a composite operation*

This isn't exactly what I intended the output image to look like, however, because I haven't specified an alpha channel in the image to be placed on top. If you add an alpha channel, then the new output image looks like Figure 4-9.

Figure 4-9. *The output image after a composite operation with a top image that has an alpha channel*

You can see from this example that the composite command will respect the alpha channel if one is defined for the image on top. (Chapter 7 discusses alpha channels in more detail.)

You can harness the composite command and transparency to add some really nice effects. For example, I get quite a few requests for details on how to create images with rounded corners, which is a style that has been made popular by Apple's Mac OS X. To do this, you need to make a rounded corner, with the transparency set up correctly so that the inside of the corner is transparent. If you want premade corners, you can download mine from http://www.stillhq.com/extracted/article-imagingtoolsmore/corners/.

I'll now show how to give the image in Figure 4-10 rounded corners.

Figure 4-10. *A bird photo with square corners*

To do this, you need to use four invocations of the composite command:

```
composite -gravity NorthEast rounded-ne.png bird.png bird-1.png
composite -gravity NorthWest rounded-nw.png bird-1.png bird-2.png
composite -gravity SouthEast rounded-se.png bird-2.png bird-3.png
composite -gravity SouthWest rounded-sw.png bird-3.png bird-4.png
```

This gives you the finished image in Figure 4-11.

Figure 4-11. *A bird photo with rounded corners*

For more discussion on the gravity command-line option used in this example, refer to Chapter 7. You can also ask the composite command to dissolve the images into each other, which can produce animations with some nice effects. For instance, let's say you have two photos of flowers, as shown in Figure 4-12 and Figure 4-13.

Figure 4-12. *The first flower*

Figure 4-13. *The second flower*

Say you want to combine these two photos with different dissolve levels. Generally, the command line you use looks like this:

```
composite -dissolve 42% input1.jpg input2.jpg output.jpg
```

This will dissolve input1.jpg into input2.jpg by 42 percent. Figure 4-14 shows some examples of various dissolve percentages.

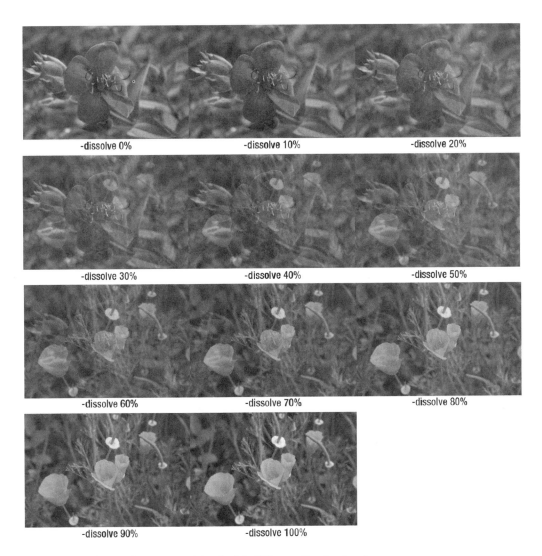

Figure 4-14. *The two images combined with different dissolve levels*

You can also combine images using the blend command-line option, which takes a percentage argument much like dissolve but produces slightly different results visually. The difference between the two operations is that the dissolve command-line option adjusts the transparency of the images before combining them, whilst the blend command uses a weighted average of the images to produce its output.

The `composite` command can also produce watermarks on images. For example, I'll now show how to place the watermark shown in Figure 4-15 on the picture of the flower from Figure 4-12.

Draft

Figure 4-15. *A watermark to apply to the image*

To do this, use this command line:

```
composite -watermark 30% watermark.png input.jpg output.jpg
```

The main difference between watermarking and dissolving or blending is that the watermark image doesn't need to be the same size as the input image. Figure 4-16 shows the output image that this command line gives you.

Figure 4-16. *The image with a watermark applied*

The problem with this image is that the watermark image doesn't have an alpha channel set; it has a white background instead, which is why it has that lighter rectangle in the image. You can fix this by making the white in the image 100 percent transparent. After that, you get the image shown in Figure 4-17.

Figure 4-17. *The image with a transparent watermark applied*

The watermark command-line option takes an argument that specifies the transparency of the watermark. Figure 4-18 shows some of the transparency values and what the results look like.

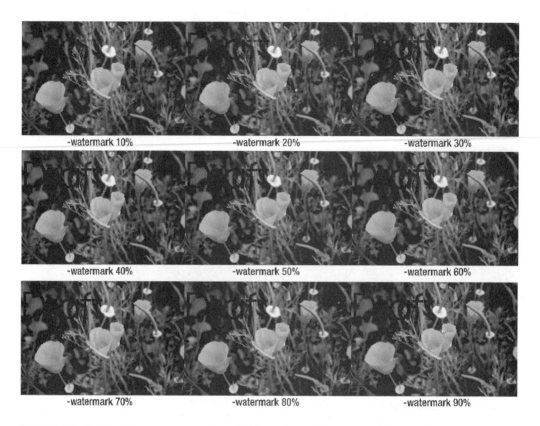

Figure 4-18. *Various transparency options for the* watermark *command-line option*

You can choose the placement of the watermark by using the gravity command-line option like this:

```
composite -watermark 30% -gravity center watermark.png input.jpg output.jpg
```

This gives you the image shown in Figure 4-19.

Figure 4-19. *A centered watermark*

Finally, for the composite command, I'll show you how to use the stegano command-line option to hide images inside other images. You can use this to determine whether an image you find on the Internet has been taken from your site (although you can also use it for passing secret messages). To hide the image, first you need an image to hide other images in, and then you need the hidden image. For this example, I'll show how to hide the image shown in Figure 4-20.

**This image is
from stillhq.com**

Figure 4-20. *An image to hide*

I'll show how to hide this inside the image shown in Figure 4-21.

Figure 4-21. *The image in which you'll hide the logo*

To do this, use this command line:

```
composite -stegano 42 logo.png input.jpg output.png
```

The argument to the `stegano` command-line option is the inset inside the input image at which to start hiding the logo. This number needs to be kept secret, or other people will be able to extract the logo. This gives you the image shown in Figure 4-22.

Figure 4-22. *The image with the logo hidden*

To extract the image again, you use the `display` command like this:

```
display -size 204x61+42 stegano:output.png
```

You should note three points about this command line. First, you need to know the size of the logo, which can be determined by using the `identify` command (which is discussed later in this chapter in the "identify" section). Second, you need to know the offset of the image within the other image. It is also important to note that this command will take quite a while to execute. On my 1.7-gigahertz Centrino laptop, this command took 51 seconds to execute. When ready, the `display` command will display the logo image. Finally, the image with the logo hidden inside it is affected by having the logo placed in it, so you need to be willing to accept some image quality loss.

How do you find stolen images using this technique? Well, it's not a good active search technique, because you'd need to perform this slow technique to every image on the Internet. If, however, you stumble across images that you suspect are from your site, then you can use this to prove the point. Unfortunately, the embedded logo might not survive transformations on the stolen image such as resizing, cropping, and so forth.

conjure

ImageMagick implements a scripting language for automating processing called the Magick Scripting Language (MSL). The `conjure` command takes these scripts in Extensible Markup Language (XML) form and executes them. The scripting language used is out the scope of this book, but Chapters 8 through 11 cover lots of other programming options. You can read more about the `conjure` command at `http://www.imagemagick.org/script/conjure.php`.

convert

The `convert` command is the subject of the majority of this book, because it contains most of the ImageMagick functionality. Therefore, I won't document the command any further here, instead referring you to the rest of the book for information. Specifically, see the following chapters: 3, 5, 6, and 7.

identify

Chapter 3 discussed the `identify` command. This command outputs interesting information about the image file (or files) that it's passed. If you're interested in only simple information about the image and want it to be returned efficiently, then you're best off using the `ping` command-line option:

```
identify -ping input.jpg
```

```
input.jpg JPEG 816x612 DirectClass 103kb 0.040u 0:01
```

You can get more information about the image if you use other command-line options. If you specify no command-line options at all, then you get similar output to the `ping` command-line option, as shown here:

```
identify input.jpg
```

```
input.jpg JPEG 816x612 DirectClass 103kb 0.040u 0:01
```

Here you can see that the image is 816×612 pixels and is JPEG compressed. If you want more information about the file, try adding the verbose command-line option:

```
identify -verbose input.jpg
```

```
input.jpg JPEG 816x612 DirectClass 103kb 0.030u 0:01
Image: input.jpg
  Format: JPEG (Joint Photographic Experts Group JFIF format)
  Geometry: 816x612
  Class: DirectClass
  Type: TrueColor
  Endianess: Undefined
  Colorspace: RGB
  Channel depth:
    Red: 8-bits
    Green: 8-bits
    Blue: 8-bits
  Channel statistics:
    Red:
      Min: 95 (0.372549)
      Max: 255 (1)
      Mean: 226.582 (0.888556)
      Standard deviation: 12.6188 (0.0494854)
    Green:
      Min: 0 (0)
      Max: 255 (1)
      Mean: 19.4916 (0.0764375)
      Standard deviation: 45.3697 (0.177921)
    Blue:
      Min: 0 (0)
      Max: 255 (1)
      Mean: 42.3754 (0.166178)
      Standard deviation: 40.5556 (0.159042)
  Colors: 31265
  Rendering-intent: Undefined
  Resolution: 72x72
  Units: PixelsPerInch
  Filesize: 103kb
  Interlace: None
  Background Color: white
  Border Color: #DFDFDF
  Matte Color: grey74
  Dispose: Undefined
  Iterations: 0
  Compression: JPEG
```

```
Quality: 80
Orientation: Undefined
JPEG-Colorspace: 2
JPEG-Sampling-factors: 2x1,1x1,1x1
Signature: 4a957426ccdc4f819c591f0f020920bef1b1ec4739fd17084bab38c617ccf83a
Profile-exif: 6140 bytes
...dump of those 6,140 bytes omitted for clarity...
    Image Description:
    Make: SONY.
    Model: CYBERSHOT U.
    Orientation: 1
    X Resolution: 72/1
    Y Resolution: 72/1
    Resolution Unit: 2
    Date Time: 2005:05:13 07:27:09.
    Y Cb Cr Positioning: 2
    Exif Offset: 220
    Exposure Time: 10/1600
    F Number: 40/10
    Exposure Program: 2
    ISO Speed Ratings: 100
    Exif Version: 0220
    Date Time Original: 2005:05:13 07:27:09.
    Date Time Digitized: 2005:05:13 07:27:09.
    Components Configuration: ....
    Compressed Bits Per Pixel: 2/1
    Exposure Bias Value: 0/10
    Max Aperture Value: 48/16
    Metering Mode: 2
    Light Source: 0
    Flash: 0
    Focal Length: 50/10
    Maker Note:
    Flash Pix Version: 0100
    Color Space: 1
    Exif Image Width: 1632
    Exif Image Length: 1224
    Interoperability Offset: 638
    Interoperability Index: R98.
    Interoperability Version: 0100
    File Source: .
    Scene Type: .
    Custom Rendered: 0
    Exposure Mode: 0
    White Balance: 0
    Scene Capture Type: 0
  Tainted: False
  Version: ImageMagick 6.2.3 06/09/05 Q16 http://www.imagemagick.org
```

You can see that this produces a lot of information about the image, including all the information embedded in the JPEG file's EXIF metadata tags (a metadata format specific to the JPEG file format). In return for seeing all this information, the command can take quite some time to complete. The `identify` command can also take a `format` argument, which gives you a chance to output only the information you want. The format of the `format` argument is identical to the format used for the `comment` command-line argument, as discussed in Chapter 3.

You can use this information in some interesting ways; for an example, check out the programming example in Chapter 8.

import

ImageMagick also ships with a screen-capture program called `import`. When you run the command, the cursor in X Windows becomes a set of crosshairs, and when you click a window, the contents of that window are saved into the specified file. For example, the following command line:

```
import capture.png
```

saves the image shown in Figure 4-23 when you click a window.

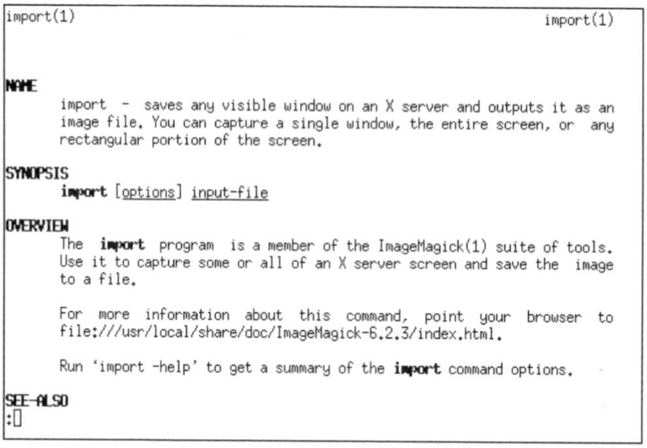

```
import(1)                                                        import(1)


NAME
       import  -  saves any visible window on an X server and outputs it as an
       image file. You can capture a single window, the entire screen, or  any
       rectangular portion of the screen.

SYNOPSIS
       import [options] input-file

OVERVIEW
       The  import  program  is a member of the ImageMagick(1) suite of tools.
       Use it to capture some or all of an X server screen and save the  image
       to a file.

       For  more  information  about  this  command,  point your  browser  to
       file:///usr/local/share/doc/ImageMagick-6.2.3/index.html.

       Run 'import -help' to get a summary of the import command options.

SEE-ALSO
:[]
```

Figure 4-23. *A captured window*

To import the frame from the window as well, use the `frame` command-line option:

```
import -frame capture.png
```

You can import more than one image at a time by specifying more than output filename on the command line:

```
import output1.png output2.png
```

If you need some delay between the image captures, you can use the `pause` command-line option, which takes the number of seconds to delay before each capture (including the first):

```
import -pause 10 output1.png output2.png
```

This produces the two captures shown in Figure 4-24 and Figure 4-25, with a total capture time of 20 seconds.

Figure 4-24. *The first captured window from the multiple import*

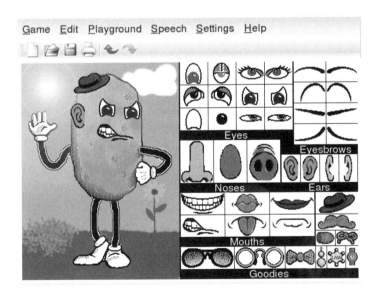

Figure 4-25. *The second captured window from the multiple import*

The import command needs an X Windows server, so unless you have one enabled on your Microsoft Windows machine, then this command won't work.

mogrify

Chapter 2 briefly introduced the mogrify command, which takes the same arguments as the convert command; however, the difference is that the mogrify command takes only one image file as an argument. Instead of saving the changed image into the second named file like the convert command does, the mogrify command will change the original image. This makes the mogrify command much more convenient for processing many images at once, because you can specify all of them on the command line, like so:

```
mogrify -implode 4 *.jpg
```

This example applies the implode effect (discussed in Chapter 5) to all the images in the current directory whose filenames end with .jpg. To achieve the same effect with the convert command, you need to implement a simple shell script:

```
for item in *.jpg
do
  convert -implode 4 $item /tmp/$item
  mv /tmp/$item $item
done
```

The convert command requires a lot more work and will be less reliable. What if you wanted to change the image format of a bunch of images? The format command-line option allows you to do this. For example, to turn a bunch of JPEG files into PNGs, you can use this command line:

```
mogrify -format png *.jpg
```

This will convert all the files in the current directory ending with .jpg into PNG files by changing the extension in the filename. This can also be handy if you want to keep the original images but want a shorthand way to apply a transformation to all those images. If you use this option, bear in mind that there can be issues associated with converting images to another format, as discussed in Chapter 3.

montage

The montage command creates an image from a sequence of images. For example, to create an image that contains thumbnails of the images it was passed, use the following command line:

```
montage *.jpg output.png
```

Figure 4-26 shows an example of the output.

Figure 4-26. *Output from the* montage *command*

The montage command can take some arguments of its own as well. For example, to label the images in the montage, use the label command-line argument. To label the images with the filename, use the following command line:

```
montage -label %f *.jpg output.png
```

This displays the output shown in Figure 4-27.

001.jpg   002.jpg   003.jpg   004.jpg   005.jpg

006.jpg   007.jpg   008.jpg   009.jpg   010.jpg

011.jpg   012.jpg   013.jpg   014.jpg   015.jpg

016.jpg   017.jpg

Figure 4-27. *Output from the* montage *command, with the* label *option*

You can find more documentation on the substitution strings to use in the label string in Chapter 3.

To put a frame around the images, you can add the frame command-line option. Here's a frame with a size of 5:

```
montage -label %f -frame 5 *.jpg output.png
```

This gives you the output shown in Figure 4-28.

Figure 4-28. *Output from the* montage *command, with the* label *option and a* frame *option of 5*

In contrast to that, Figure 4-29 shows a frame with a size of 1.

Figure 4-29. *Output from the* montage *command, with the* label *option and a* frame *option of 1*

Apart from frames, you can also create shadows around the images by using the shadow command-line option. Here's an example:

```
montage -label %f -shadow *.jpg output.png
```

ImageMagick creates the image shown in Figure 4-30.

Figure 4-30. *Output of the* montage *command, with a shadow*

You can combine the shadow effect with a frame, like this:

```
montage -label %f -shadow -frame 5*.jpg output.png
```

You get the effect shown in Figure 4-31.

Figure 4-31. *Output of the* montage *command, with a shadow and a frame*

Many of the color and stroke options discussed in Chapter 7 affect the way frames are drawn. For example, you can use the border color, background color, fill color, and stroke color to change features such as the background color of the image and the way the frame is painted. Experiment with these options if you'd like to further customize the way frames in montages look. The montage command can even create HTML image maps; however, since image maps are a bit dated as a concept now, I won't cover them in this chapter.

You can also manipulate the space that each thumbnail consumes. For instance, to enforce a 100×200 space for each thumbnail image, you can use this command line:

```
montage -label %f -frame 5 -geometry 100x200 *.jpg output.png
```

This produces the output shown in Figure 4-32.

Figure 4-32. *Output from the* montage *command, with the* label *option, a* frame *option of 1, and a given frame size enforced*

You can find more information about the geometry command-line option in Chapter 2. I'll briefly show you how to add space around images, though. You do this with a geometry that consists of a plus sign and the horizontal spacing and a plus sign and the vertical spacing. For example, to put 10 pixels of horizontal spacing and 5 pixels of vertical spacing around an image, use a command line like this:

```
montage -label %f -frame 5 -geometry +10+5 *.jpg output.png
```

This gives you the image shown in Figure 4-33.

Figure 4-33. *Output from the* montage *command, with the* label *option, a* frame *option of 1, and spacing enforced*

You can create gaps in the montage by using the special null filename:

```
montage 001.jpg null: 002.jpg output.png
```

This gives you a montage with a blank space in the middle, as shown in Figure 4-34.

Figure 4-34. *A montage with a gap*

Furthermore, you can label some images and not others by using the `label` command-line option to specify a label and then use the `+label` command-line option to turn labels off:

```
montage -label "An image" 001.jpg +label null: -label "Another image" ➥
002.jpg output.png
```

This gives you an image with a gap in the middle and no label for the gap, as shown in Figure 4-35.

An image   Another image

Figure 4-35. *An example of not labeling all images*

Finally, you can tell the `montage` command how many images to have per row in the output. You do this with the `tile` command-line option, which lets you specify the maximum number of thumbnails to appear in a row. For example, to enforce having three thumbnails in each row, you can use the following command line (which also uses some of the examples described previously):

```
montage -label %f -frame 5 -tile 3 *.jpg output.png
```

This produces the output shown in Figure 4-36.

Figure 4-36. *Output from the* montage *command, with the* label *option, a* frame *option of 1, and a maximum of three thumbnails per row*

If you want to specify the number of rows, then you can specify a grid like this:

```
montage -label %f -frame 5 -tile 5x5 *.jpg output.png
```

This produces the output shown in Figure 4-37.

Figure 4-37. *Output from the montage, having specified a number of output rows*

This example has a blank line at the bottom, because you told ImageMagick you wanted five output rows, even though only four were needed. To tell ImageMagick to work out how many images to put in each row and specify only the number of output rows, then just specify that number with an x at the front:

```
montage -label %f -frame 5 -tile x5 *.jpg output.png
```

ImageMagick works out how many images should go in each of the five rows and creates the montage shown in Figure 4-38.

Figure 4-38. *Output from montage, having specified a number of output rows but not the number of images in each row*

Using the Graphical Tools

Along with the command-line tools you've seen so far, ImageMagick ships with a variety of graphical tools. These graphical tools require an X Windows server to work, which can make them harder to use on Microsoft Windows machines. If you're running Windows, then I recommend looking into installing an X Windows server if these tools sound interesting.

animate

The animate command displays either an animated file, such as an animated GIF file, or a sequence of image files as an animation in a window. If you're using Microsoft Windows, then you need to have an X Windows server installed for this command to work. Figure 4-39 shows an example of `animate` in action; it displays a set of images from Chapter 5 of this book.

Figure 4-39. *The* animate *command running*

The `animate` command also has a graphical menu that will appear if you click the image. Figure 4-40 shows what the menu looks like.

Figure 4-40. *The* animate *command's menu*

Click any of these buttons to be prompted for what you'd like `animate` to do. Options include controlling what animation you're viewing, setting the direction of the animation (forward or backward), setting the speed of the animation, and getting information on the images being viewed. You can also access help from within the application. Right-click the image to make the menu disappear. The information about the images is the repackaged output of the `identify` command, which looks like Figure 4-41 when displayed by `animate`.

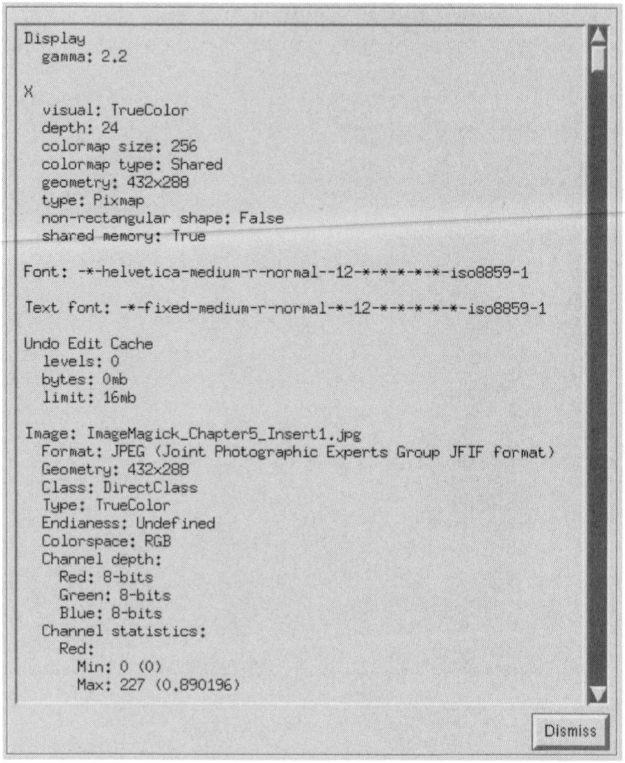

```
Display
   gamma: 2.2

X
   visual: TrueColor
   depth: 24
   colormap size: 256
   colormap type: Shared
   geometry: 432x288
   type: Pixmap
   non-rectangular shape: False
   shared memory: True

Font: -*-helvetica-medium-r-normal--12-*-*-*-*-*-iso8859-1

Text font: -*-fixed-medium-r-normal-*-12-*-*-*-*-*-iso8859-1

Undo Edit Cache
   levels: 0
   bytes: 0mb
   limit: 16mb

Image: ImageMagick_Chapter5_Insert1.jpg
   Format: JPEG (Joint Photographic Experts Group JFIF format)
   Geometry: 432x288
   Class: DirectClass
   Type: TrueColor
   Endianess: Undefined
   Colorspace: RGB
   Channel depth:
      Red: 8-bits
      Green: 8-bits
      Blue: 8-bits
   Channel statistics:
      Red:
         Min: 0 (0)
         Max: 227 (0.890196)

                                                    Dismiss
```

Figure 4-41. *The* animate *command displaying information about some images*

display

The display command is the other graphical command implemented by ImageMagick, which also requires an X Windows server. If you're using Microsoft Windows, then you'll need to install such an X Windows server before this command will work. When invoked with an image filename, display simply displays the image on the screen. You can also include the backdrop command-line option to tell display to display the image centered on the screen, with the rest of the screen being covered in a neutral backdrop. For example:

display -backdrop image.png

To specify the color of the backdrop, you can set the background color like this:

display -background green -backdrop image.png

You can find more information about how to specify colors in Chapter 7.

Furthermore, display can automatically watch files when they're being displayed and redisplay them if they change on disk. This can come in handy if you have an automated process that produces an image and you want to keep and eye on it, such as when displaying on your desktop what your Web camera is currently sending to the Internet. You implement this with the update command-line option:

display -update 5 input.jpg

This will tell `display` to check whether the `input.jpg` file has changed on disk every five seconds and redisplay it if it has. You can also change the title of the window that the `display` command uses with the `title` command-line option:

```
display -title "This is a picture of a foo" input.jpg
```

This command-line option also works for the `animate` and `montage` commands. You can include information about the image in this string as well as use the format strings discussed in Chapter 3.

Finally, for the `display` command line, you can tell the command to display the image as the background for a given X window. For this to happen, just specify the window ID to use:

```
display -window root image.png
```

This sets your desktop pattern to the image in `image.png`. You can also specify the individual ID of an X window. To get the ID of a window, use the `xwininfo` command. This command will turn your mouse cursor into a set of crosshairs, and when you click a window, it will dump useful information such as this:

```
xwininfo: Please select the window about which you
          would like information by clicking the
          mouse in that window.

xwininfo: Window id: 0x2600010 ➡
"mikal@challenger: /home/mikal/imagemagickbook/content"

  Absolute upper-left X:  21
  Absolute upper-left Y:  478
  Relative upper-left X:  4
  Relative upper-left Y:  21
  Width: 772
  Height: 511
  Depth: 24
  Visual Class: TrueColor
  Border width: 0
  Class: InputOutput
  Colormap: 0x20 (installed)
  Bit Gravity State: NorthWestGravity
  Window Gravity State: NorthWestGravity
  Backing Store State: NotUseful
  Save Under State: no
  Map State: IsViewable
  Override Redirect State: no
  Corners:  +21+478  -607+478  -607-61  +21-61
  -geometry 128x39+17-57
```

This is similar to how the `import` command works.

When you have an image being displayed that isn't the background of an X window, if you click the image, a menu appears with a number of options. Figure 4-42 shows this menu.

Figure 4-42. *The display menu*

The File menu lets you access the functions you'd expect from such a menu, such as opening new files, moving the next file in a list provided on the command line, moving to a previous file listed on the command line, saving your changes, printing, and so forth.

The Edit menu supplies undo and redo facilities, as well as cut and paste. The View menu lets you change the size at which the image is displayed, apply changes, and refresh the image.

The Transform, Enhance, F/X, Image Edit, and Miscellany menus let you perform many of the transformations covered in this book. These menus provide you with an interactive method of determining which transformations to perform in which order to get the result you desire. You can also apply these preview transformations with the preview command-line option. See the ImageMagick documentation at http://www.imagemagick.org/script/display.php.

The Help menu provides online help. Right-click the image for a list of shortcuts.

Conclusion

In this chapter, you looked at the various command-line and graphical tools that ImageMagick provides. The convert command is the focus of most of this book, so refer to other chapters for more information about it. Specifically, see Chapter 2, Chapter 3, Chapter 5, and Chapter 6.

ImageMagick can perform a lot of useful functions with the commands it provides, including creating montages of images with a large variety of formatting options, displaying your images for you, capturing windows from your X Windows session, and displaying images as the background in those windows on your X session. ImageMagick can perform many functions that aren't covered by the convert command, and this chapter has shown you a few of them. I could show you other details about these commands, but it would take hundreds of pages to do so. I recommend you refer to the ImageMagick documentation at http://www.imagemagick.org if you need more specific details of a command that you've seen in this chapter.

The next chapter shows you some of the more artistic transformations that ImageMagick can perform, and Chapter 6 shows you the remainder of the image transformations ImageMagick offers. Chapter 7 covers how to draw on existing images and create new images with ImageMagick; then I'll move introduce four examples of programmer interfaces to ImageMagick, so read on for more details.

CHAPTER 5

■ ■ ■

Performing Artistic Transformations

The approach for this chapter is slightly different from the approach you've seen in previous chapters. This chapter discusses some of the artistic transformations available with the convert command. These transformations all take arguments that affect the amount of transformation applied, so for each transformation I'll provide a number of examples with different arguments to make this clearer. For these examples, I'll use the image shown in Figure 5-1 to make the transformations more apparent.

Figure 5-1. *The input image for the examples in this chapter*

Additionally, I'll briefly describe each transformation and what it's doing to the image. I recommend you refer to the ImageMagick documentation at http://www.imagemagick.org for more information if you need to know more than what is included here.

blur

The blur command-line option applies a Gaussian–function-based blurring operation to the image. This command-line option is also called gaussian. The argument is the radius of the blur, with an optional standard deviation. To specify just a radius, use the following version of the command:

```
convert -blur 12 input.jpg output.jpg
```

To specify a standard deviation as well, use the following:

```
convert -blur 12x2 input.jpg output.jpg
```

This command specifies that a blur with radius of 12 and a standard deviation of 2 be used. Figure 5-2 shows some examples of the blur command's output with no standard deviation specified.

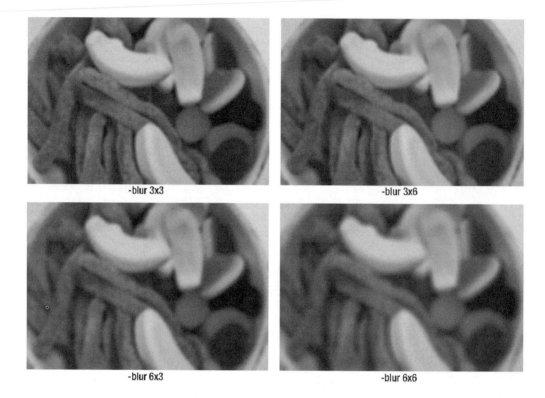

-blur 3x3   -blur 3x6

-blur 6x3   -blur 6x6

Figure 5-2. *Various* blur *sizes with no standard deviation*

A more detailed discussion of the Gaussian function is outside the scope of this book but will be covered in a good math textbook. Alternatively, http://en.wikipedia.org/wiki/ Gaussian_function provides a good introduction.

charcoal

The next transformation I'll show you is the charcoal command-line option. This option simulates a charcoal drawing by finding the color boundaries in the image and then reinforcing those boundaries with thick, dark lines. Additionally, the transformation uses a grayscale effect for the body of colors. The transformation takes one argument, which is the thickness of the lines to draw. For example, to produce a simple image, use the following command:

```
convert -charcoal 4 input.jpg output.jpg
```

Figure 5-3 shows a bunch of examples of the charcoal effect with different arguments. This can be an appealing effect visually.

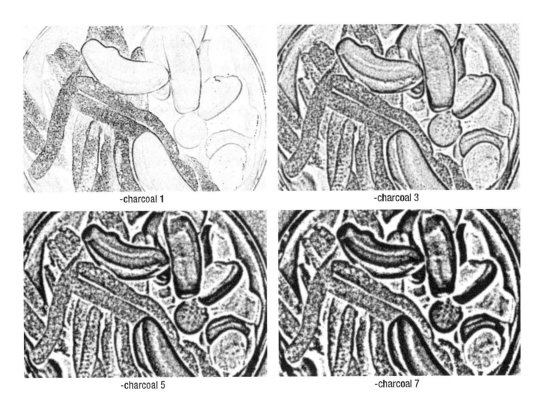

Figure 5-3. *The charcoal effect with various arguments*

colorize

The colorize command uses the fill color currently specified and adds a specified percentage of that color to the image being processed. For example, this command line:

```
convert -colorize 10 input.jpg output.jpg
```

adds a 10 percent share of the current fill color (the default in this example, which is black) to the image. Progressively adding more gives a nice fade-out effect, as demonstrated in Figure 5-4.

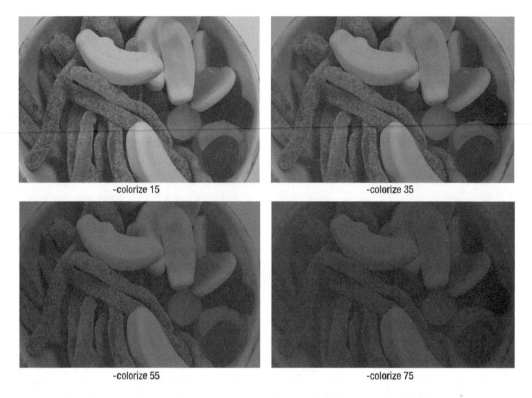

Figure 5-4. *Colorizing an image with different intensities, using the default black fill color*

You can also specify a different fill color. You just use the `fill` command-line option, which is discussed more in Chapter 7. The following command line specifies a blue fill color:

```
convert -fill blue -colorize 10 input.jpg output.jpg
```

You can find out more about how to specify colors in ImageMagick in Chapters 1 and 7. Figure 5-5 shows this command line with a variety of `colorize` values.

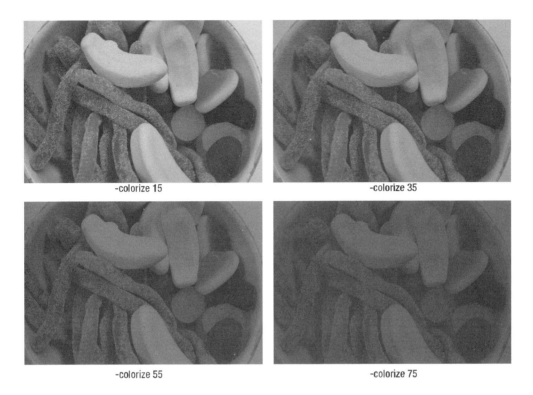

Figure 5-5. *Colorizing an image using a blue fill color*

You can also just colorize one image channel. Specify the colorize value for each channel like this:

```
convert -colorize 10/20/30 input.jpg output.jpg
```

This example will colorize the red channel by 10 percent, the green channel by 20 percent, and the blue channel by 30 percent. The comparison in Figure 5-6 applies varying colorize levels to just the red channel of the image.

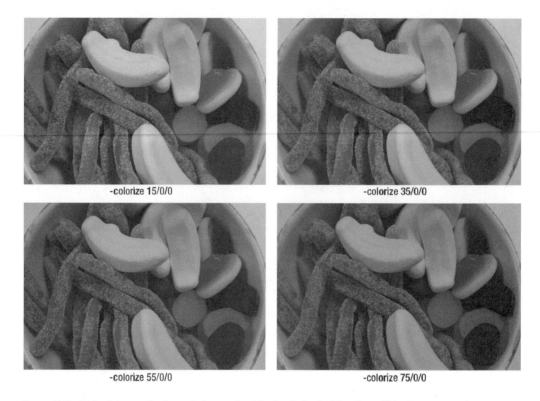

Figure 5-6. *Colorizing only the red channel with the default fill color of black*

implode

The implode transformation makes it look like the center of the image has been sucked into a black hole in the middle of the image. The implode command takes one argument, which is the factor by which to apply the effect. The size of the effect on the image is that factor argument. For example, to implode an image by 10, use a command line like this:

```
convert -implode 10 input.jpg output.jpg
```

Figure 5-7 shows the implode effect with various factor sizes.

Figure 5-7. *The implode effect with various factor sizes*

noise

The noise transformation either removes or adds noise to an image, optionally using different methods to determine what is noise in the image. The most common use for this transform is to "smooth out" images if they have slight imperfections. This is one example of the noise command:

```
convert -noise 3 input.jpg output.jpg
```

For example, Figure 5-8 shows the effect of the noise command with various numeric arguments.

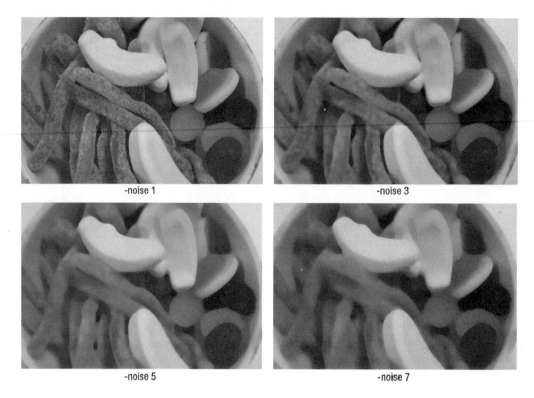

Figure 5-8. *The noise effect with various radii*

The numeric argument is the radius over which to remove the noise per pixel. *Noise* is defined as being an extreme maximum or minimum value within that radius, so the size of the radius produces dramatically different effects on the image.

You can also use the noise transformation to add noise to an image. To show how this works, I'll start with the image in Figure 5-9, which is a solid color.

Figure 5-9. *A solid color*

This is actually light blue, although the printing process doesn't make that apparent. These are the types of noise you can add to the image:

- Uniform

- Gaussian

- Multiplicative

- Impulse

- Laplacian

- Poisson

You add the noise with a command line like this, which adds Gaussian noise:

```
convert +noise Gaussian input.jpg output.jpg
```

Figure 5-10 shows the new image, with the various types of noise applied.

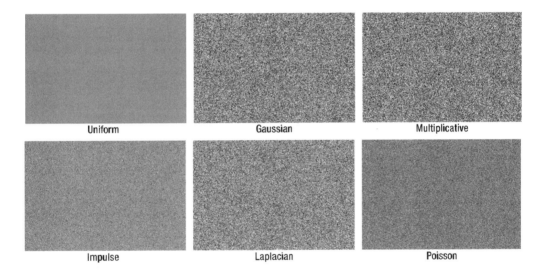

Figure 5-10. *Various types of added noise*

Figure 5-11 shows the photo I've used in earlier examples in this chapter with the various types of noise added.

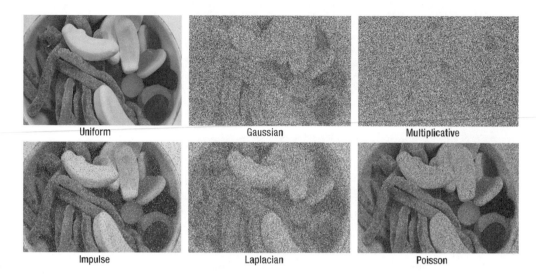

Figure 5-11. *Various types of added noise to the example photograph*

paint

One of the most visually attractive transformations that ImageMagick offers is the paint effect. The paint effect simulates an oil painting by replacing the color of a pixel with the most common color in a circular area that is specified by the radius argument to the command. For example, to simulate oil painting, you might pick a radius of 7 pixels and use the following command:

```
convert -paint 7 input.jpg output.jpg
```

Figure 5-12 shows a variety of radii applied with the paint command.

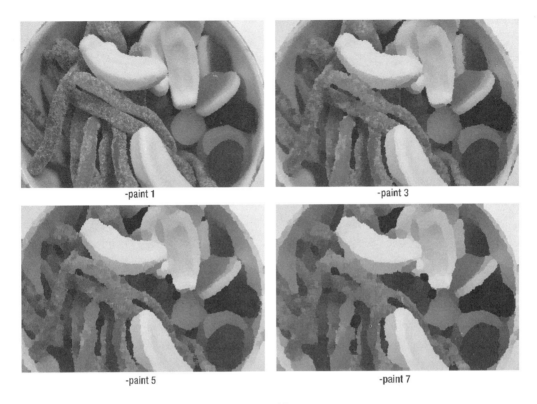

Figure 5-12. *The* paint *command with various radii*

radial-blur

The radial blur effect is implemented with the radial-blur command-line option to the convert command. This effect rotates the image in a blurring manner around the center of the image by the number of degrees specified on the command line. The blurring motion is more notice-able at the outside of the image compared to the center. To blur an image by 45 degrees, use the following command line:

```
convert -radial-blur 45 input.jpg output.jpg
```

Figure 5-13 shows the effect of using a few different angles.

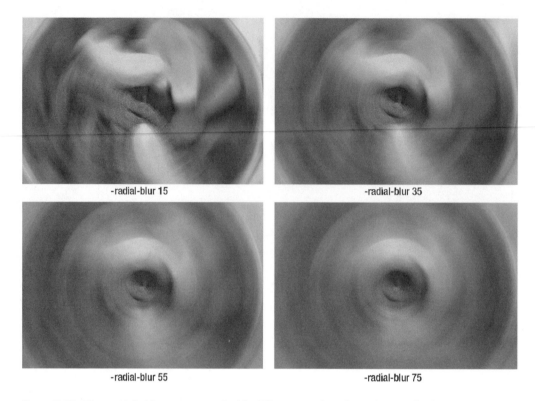

Figure 5-13. *The* radial-blur *command with different angles of rotation applied*

raise

The raise effect provides beveled edges for your image. You can specify the height and width for this bevel, as well as a direction for the bevel. To specify a different vertical bevel size from the horizontal one, you use this command line:

```
convert -raise 2x3 input.jpg output.jpg
```

This specifies a horizontal bevel of 2 pixels and a vertical bevel size of 3 pixels. Figure 5-14 shows some examples of various bevel sizes.

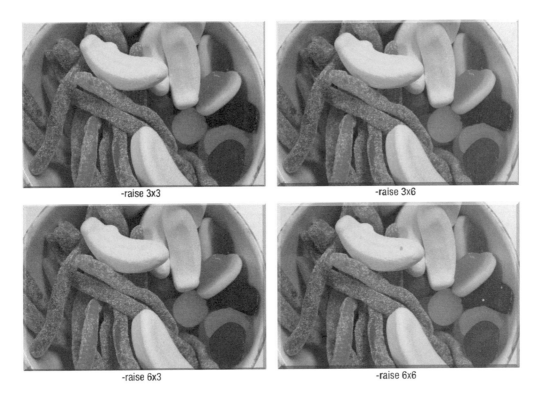

Figure 5-14. *Various bevel sizes*

To make the bevel in the other direction, then use a plus sign instead of a minus sign for the first character of the command-line option:

```
convert +raise 2x3 input.jpg output.jpg
```

This command gives you the images shown in Figure 5-15.

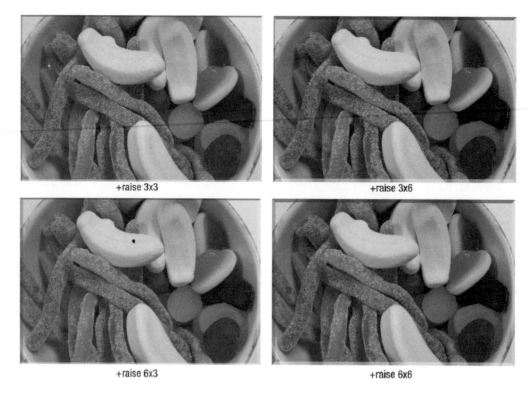

Figure 5-15. *Various bevel sizes, in the other direction*

segment

The segment transformation uses histograms of each color component to determine which colors are homogenous, and then it combines those colors. Two arguments are available for this transformation—the clustering threshold and the smoothing threshold. The clustering threshold controls how different colors need to be to avoid being clustered together, and the smoothing threshold eliminates noise in the second derivative of the histogram. The default value for the smoothing threshold is 1.5.

Accurately describing this transformation is a fairly technical field that is really outside the scope of this book, so if you need to know more than this, please refer to the ImageMagick documentation at http://www.imagemagick.org. The transformation does produce visually appealing results, though.

To use the default smoothing threshold, just specify a clustering threshold like this:

```
convert -segment 2 input.jpg output.jpg
```

To specify both clustering and smoothing, then use a command line like this:

```
convert -segment 2x3 input.jpg output.jpg
```

where the clustering threshold is 2 and the smoothing threshold is 3. Figure 5-16 shows some example results.

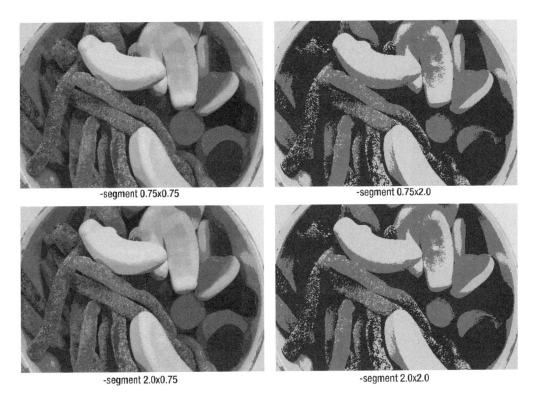

-segment 0.75x0.75   -segment 0.75x2.0

-segment 2.0x0.75   -segment 2.0x2.0

Figure 5-16. *Example uses of the segment transformation*

sepia-tone

The sepia tone effect applied via the `sepia-tone` command-line option simulates the old sepia-toned photos you sometimes see. The effect has a threshold at which to start applying the tone effect. The recommended starting point is 80 percent, as shown in the following command line:

```
convert -sepia-tone 80% input.jpg output.jpg
```

Figure 5-17 shows a variety of percentages being applied to the comparison image.

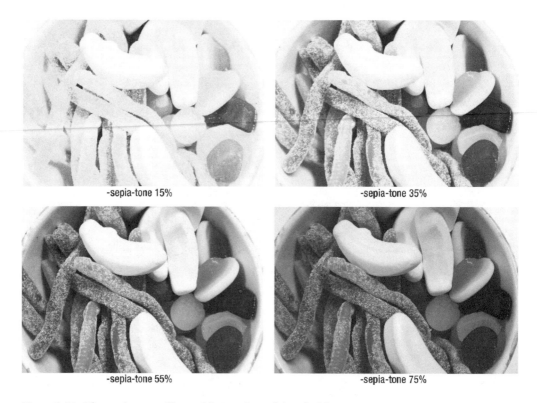

-sepia-tone 15%

-sepia-tone 35%

-sepia-tone 55%

-sepia-tone 75%

Figure 5-17. *The sepia tone effect, with a variety of threshold percentages*

shade

The shade effect simulates having a distant light source casting a shadow on the image. You can create this effect by specifying an azimuth and elevation for the light source. The *azimuth* is the angle of the light source, with north being 0 degrees, east being 90 degrees, and so on. The *elevation* is the height of the light source. For example, to specify light from the east at a height of 100, use this command line:

```
convert -shade 90x100 input.jpg output.jpg
```

Figure 5-18 shows some examples.

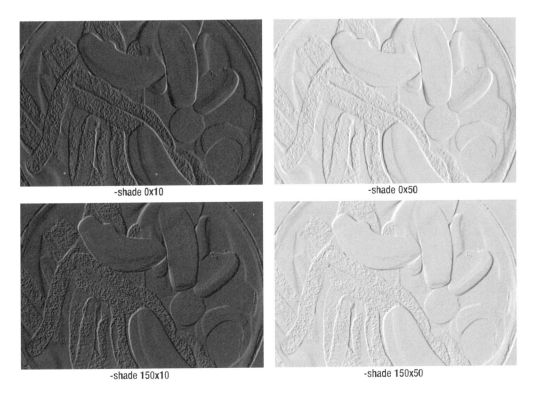

Figure 5-18. *Some examples of the shade transformation*

sharpen

The sharpen command attempts to make the color boundaries in an image more defined by using a Gaussian function. Like the blur command mentioned earlier, which also uses a Gaussian function, this command takes both a radius and an optional standard deviation. To just specify a radius, you use a command line like this:

```
convert -sharpen 3 input.jpg output.jpg
```

To specify a standard deviation, use a command line like this:

```
convert -sharpen 3x3 input.jpg output.jpg
```

Figure 5-19 shows a variety of options applied to the sample image.

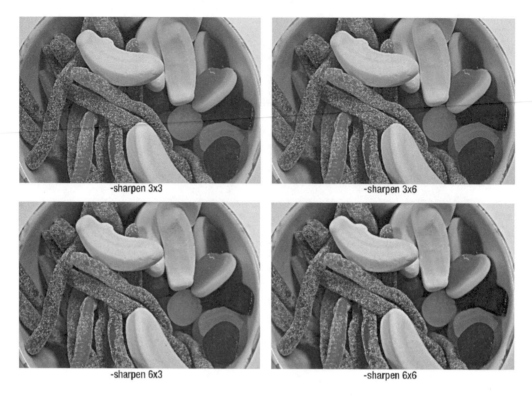

Figure 5-19. *The* sharpen *command with a variety of radii and standard deviations*

solarize

Another transformation you can apply to images is the solarize effect. This has a similar effect to exposing film negatives to light during development. It works by specifying a threshold as a percentage of the total intensity possible for the image above which the pixel will be negated. (In other words, a large value will become a small value, and a small value will become a large value.) For example, to negate all the pixels that are greater than 90 percent, use the following command:

```
convert -solarize 90 input.jpg output.jpg
```

Figure 5-20 shows the effect of various values for the solarize command on the example image.

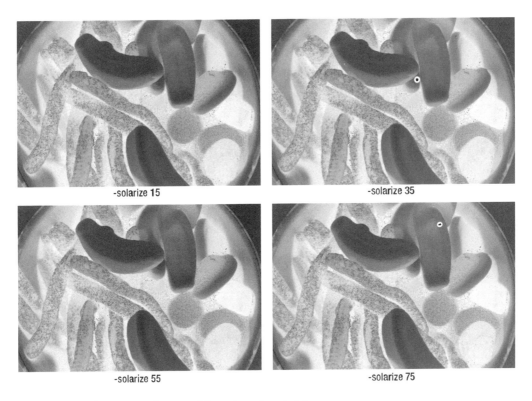

-solarize 15

-solarize 35

-solarize 55

-solarize 75

Figure 5-20. *Solarizing an image with various thresholds*

spread

Spread takes a random pixel and swaps it with the pixel that is currently being examined. This produces some really visually pleasing images with a relatively simple transformation. The transformation takes one argument—the radius of the circle around the pixel being examined in order to select the pixel with which to swap. For example, to create a spread image where the pixels are relatively close to their original locations, you might choose to use the following command line:

```
convert -spread 3 input.jpg output.jpg
```

Figure 5-21 shows a variety of radii being applied to the sample image.

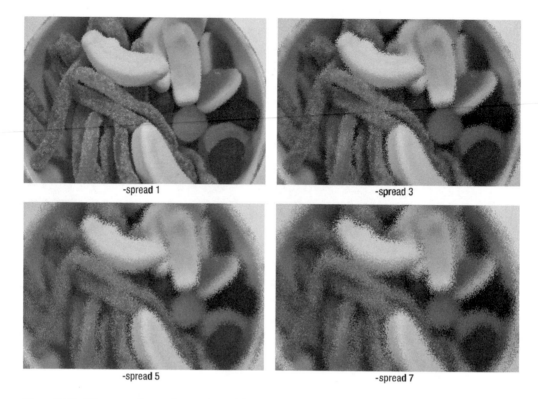

Figure 5-21. *The spread transformation with a variety of radii*

swirl

Another type of rotation effect that is quite similar to the radial blur effect is the swirl effect. swirl also rotates the image around the center for a specified number of degrees but does so without the blurring associated with the radial blur transformation. For example, to swirl an image 45 degrees, you use this command line:

```
convert -swirl 45 input.jpg output.jpg
```

Figure 5-22 shows some examples of swirls with differing amounts of rotation.

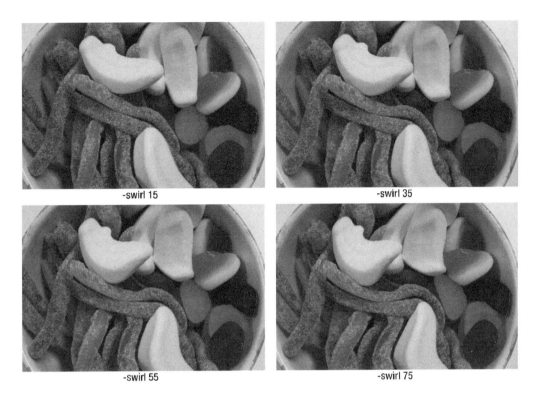

Figure 5-22. `swirl` *with different arguments*

threshold

The `threshold` transformation limits the maximum value for a given channel or all channels. For example, if you want to limit the maximum intensity of the red channel to 80 percent of its possible value, you use a command line like this:

```
convert -threshold 80,100,100% input.jpg output.jpg
```

This will just affect the red channel. To limit all channels, use the following command line:

```
convert -threshold 80% input.jpg output.jpg
```

Figure 5-23 shows the result of limiting all channels using various `threshold` commands.

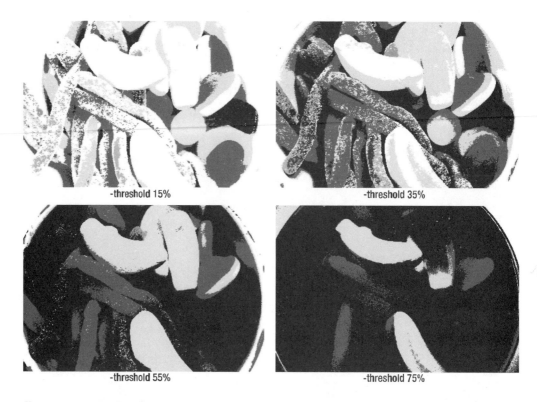

-threshold 15%

-threshold 35%

-threshold 55%

-threshold 75%

Figure 5-23. *A variety of examples of limiting all channels using the* threshold *command*

You can also specify absolute values—just omit the percentage sign. Remember also that you can apply a threshold to a single channel only.

unsharp

Confusingly, the unsharp command-line option sharpens images. Many commercial scanners use the unsharp transformation to sharpen an image just before saving it to disk. In fact, it's the recommended sharpening transformation for photographic images. The unsharp transformation was originally used by photographers; they would use an out-of-focus version of a photograph as well as the in-focus version when developing a print to give extra detail to the final image.

The unsharp transformation is very flexible; you can specify the radius of a comparison circle, the standard deviation desired, the amount of blur image to add to the image, and the threshold needed to cause the blur image to be added (expressed as a fraction of the maximum RGB value for the pixel). This is the format for these arguments:

```
convert -unsharp <radius>x<standard deviation>+<amount>+<threshold>
```

Therefore, to use the transformation with a radius of 3, a standard deviation of 1, an amount of 1.0, and a threshold of 0.05, use this command line:

```
convert -unsharp 3x1+1.0+0.05
```

The default value for the standard deviation is 1. The default value for the amount is 1.0. The default value for the threshold is 0.05 if these values aren't specified. It's recommended that the radius be larger than the standard deviation. A radius of 0 will tell ImageMagick to select an appropriate value.

The comparison images in Figure 5-24 use a variety of values for the radius and the standard deviation.

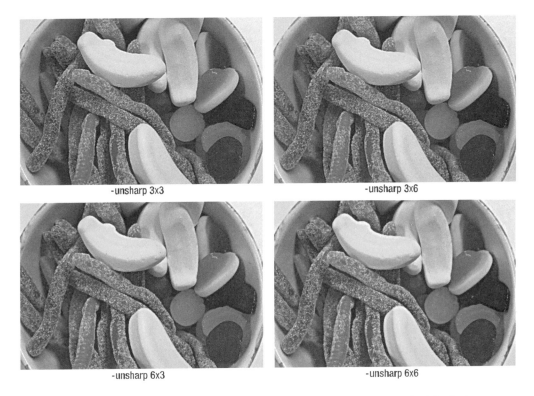

-unsharp 3x3   -unsharp 3x6

-unsharp 6x3   -unsharp 6x6

Figure 5-24. *The* unsharp *command applied with a variety of radii and standard deviations*

Next, the comparison images in Figure 5-25 use a varying amount of blurred image added to the final image.

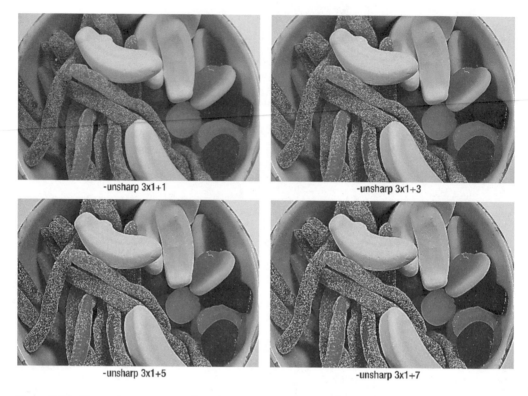

-unsharp 3x1+1   -unsharp 3x1+3

-unsharp 3x1+5   -unsharp 3x1+7

Figure 5-25. *The* unsharp *command with varying levels of blurred image added*

Finally, the comparison images in Figure 5-26 use varying thresholds.

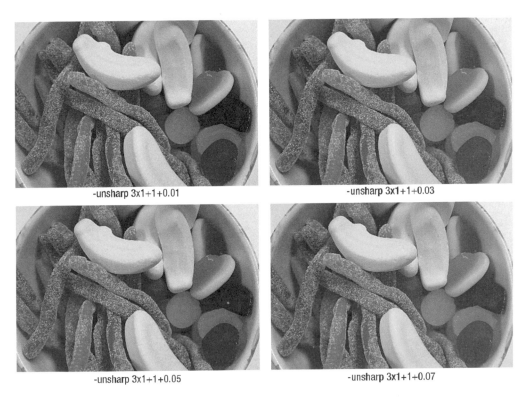

-unsharp 3x1+1+0.01

-unsharp 3x1+1+0.03

-unsharp 3x1+1+0.05

-unsharp 3x1+1+0.07

Figure 5-26. *The* unsharp *command with varying levels of threshold*

To work out what is best for your image, you should experiment until you get the effect desired.

wave

Finally, the wave transformation uses a sine wave to modify an image. A sine wave looks like Figure 5-27.

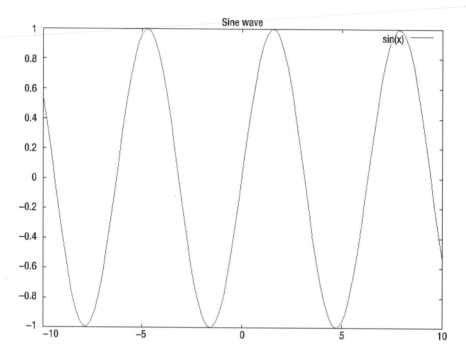

Figure 5-27. *A sine wave*

If you're not familiar with the sine wave, you can find more information about it at http://en.wikipedia.org/wiki/Sine and http://en.wikipedia.org/wiki/Sine_wave. Mathematically, the sine wave determines the size of angles within a triangle of defined edge sizes. Two factors affect the shape of this wave—the amplitude, which is the height of the wave, and the frequency, which is how wide an individual iteration of the wave is. These are the two factors that affect the wave transformation that ImageMagick offers as well. For example, to specify an amplitude of 2 and a frequency of 3, use the following command line:

```
convert -wave 2x3 input.jpg output.jpg
```

Figure 5-28 shows some examples with different amplitudes and frequencies.

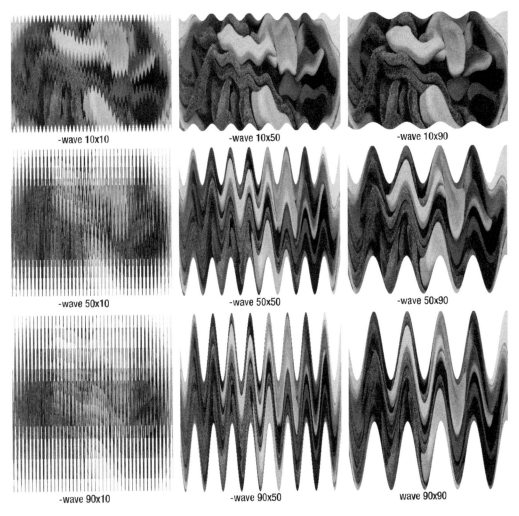

Figure 5-28. *The effect of applying the wave transformation with different amplitudes and frequencies*

virtual-pixel

Some of the transformations I've discussed in this chapter use the pixels around a given pixel to determine what to do to that pixel. In these examples, when a pixel on the edge of the input image is being examined, then ImageMagick needs to decide what to do with the missing values from that area around the pixel being examined. You can specify this behavior with the virtual-pixel command-line option. The possible values are as follows:

- `Constant`: The background color for the image will be used.

- `Edge`: The pixel on the edge of the image will be used (the default).

- `Mirror`: The image is mirrored around the edges.

- `Tile`: The image is tiled.

Transformations that use this value are the blur, sharpen, and wave transformations.

Conclusion

In this chapter, I covered some of the artistic transformations that ImageMagick lets you apply to images. Read on for information on the remaining operations I haven't covered yet, including other image transformations, drawing facilities, and various programming interfaces.

CHAPTER 6

■■■

Performing Other Image Transformations

ImageMagick can do many other image transformations that are a bit more mundane than those in the previous chapter but that are still useful. This chapter is devoted to those routine but useful transformations. I'll demonstrate the transformations with a variety of input images, and I'll discuss the available options along the way.

Performing Transformations on One Image

The following sections cover transformations you can perform on one image at a time.

Adding Borders to an Image

A commonly requested operation that ImageMagick can help you with is creating borders on images. To make simple, single-colored borders, you just use the border command-line option. This option takes two arguments—the horizontal width of the border and the vertical height of the border. For this example, I'll show how to put a 5×10-pixel border around an image. This will result in the image being 10 pixels wider and 20 pixels higher than it was before. The command line to do this is as follows:

```
convert -border 5x10 input.jpg output.jpg
```

The finished product looks like Figure 6-1.

Figure 6-1. *A photo of a koala from an Australian zoo with a gray border*

You can specify the color of the border by using the bordercolor command-line option. For example, if you want to make the border green, then you use the following command line:

```
convert -bordercolor green -border 5x10 input.jpg output.jpg
```

This gives you the image shown in Figure 6-2.

Figure 6-2. *A photo of a koala from an Australian zoo with a green border*

If you want the width and height of the border to be the same, then just use one number in the command line. For example, the following:

```
convert -border 5 input.jpg output.jpg
```

is the same as this:

```
convert -border 5x5 input.jpg output.jpg
```

Rotating an Image

It's really useful to be able to rotate images. When I empty my digital camera, for instance, I have a script that rotates the images to the correct orientation based on the information that my camera encodes into the JPEG file about the camera's orientation at the time each photo was taken. (You'll see that script in Chapter 8.) You can rotate images from the command line with ease with ImageMagick, however, by using the `rotate` command-line option.

The `rotate` command-line option takes one argument, which is the number of degrees by which to rotate the image. A positive number is the number of degrees to the right, and a negative number is the number of degrees to the left.

For example, Figure 6-3 shows a random picture from my photo collection.

Figure 6-3. *The original picture of a flower*

To rotate this picture 45 degrees to the left, use the following command line:

```
convert -rotate -45 input.jpg output.jpg
```

This gives you the image shown in Figure 6-4.

Figure 6-4. *The picture of a flower rotated 45 degrees to the left*

Rotating the image 30 degrees to the right requires the following command line:

```
convert -rotate 30 input.jpg output.jpg
```

This gives you the image shown in Figure 6-5.

Figure 6-5. *The picture of a flower rotated 30 degrees to the right*

You can also apply conditional schematics to the rotation by adding a greater-than or less-than sign to the argument. For example, to rotate the image only if its width is greater than its height, then add a greater-than sign:

```
convert -rotate -15> input.jpg output.jpg
```

To perform the inverse and rotate only if its height is greater than its width, use a less-than sign:

```
convert -rotate 60< input.jpg output.jpg
```

Remember that depending on your operating system and the shell you use, greater-than and less-than signs might be interpreted as shell commands. If they are, then you'll need to escape them using whatever mechanism your shell uses.

Finally, when you rotate an image, you create triangles in the corners. You can fill these triangles with the `background` command-line argument, which is discussed more fully in Chapter 7. Here's a simple example, though:

```
convert -background red -rotate 30 input.jpg output.jpg
```

This gives you the image shown in Figure 6-6.

Figure 6-6. *The picture of a flower rotated 30 degrees to the right with filled red corners*

Manipulating Contrast

ImageMagick can manipulate the amount of contrast in an image, either by adding more contrast to images or by reducing it. To add more contrast to an image, use the `contrast` command-line option:

```
convert -contrast input.jpg output.jpg
```

If you need to add even more contrast, then specify the command-line option more than once. For example:

```
convert -contrast -contrast input.jpg output.jpg
```

This adds even more contrast than the previous example. Figure 6-7 shows what happens to this image when you add more contrast.

Figure 6-7. *The picture of a flower with contrast added*

From top to bottom, Figure 6-8 shows the result of one contrast operation being used, then two being used, and then three being used.

You can also reduce the contrast present in an image. To do this, use a plus sign as the first character of the command-line option instead of a minus sign, like this:

```
convert +contrast input.jpg output.jpg
```

Again, specifying more than one occurrence of the +contrast command-line option will result in the effect of the operation being more pronounced. Figure 6-9 shows the same image as in Figure 6-8 but with decreasing levels of contrast.

Figure 6-8. *The picture of a flower, with increasing amounts of contrast added*

Figure 6-9. *The picture of a flower, with decreasing levels of contrast*

Dithering an Image

Dithering reduces the number of colors in an image. The most common example in everyday use is turning color images into strict black-and-white images for use in newspapers. Dithering works in a monochrome context by determining the brightness of a given color and then using the right frequency of black dots per area to imply that brightness. To demonstrate dithering, I'll use the picture of a flower shown in Figure 6-10.

Figure 6-10. *The original picture of a flower*

To dither this image into monochrome, you use a command line like this:

```
convert -dither -monochrome input.jpg output.jpg
```

This gives you the output shown in Figure 6-11.

Figure 6-11. *The picture of a flower, dithered into monochrome*

You don't have to dither to monochrome, though—you can also dither to different numbers of colors using the `colors` command-line option discussed in Chapter 2. For example, this command limits the picture to using eight colors:

```
convert -dither -colors 8 input.jpg output.jpg
```

This command line gives you the picture shown in Figure 6-12.

Figure 6-12. *The picture of a flower, dithered to use only eight colors*

To use the `dither` command-line option, you must specify either the `monochrome` command-line option or the `colors` command-line option.

Equalizing an Image

ImageMagick can also apply histogram equalization to an image. For this example, I'll show how to equalize the image shown in Figure 6-13.

Figure 6-13. *The original image to equalize*

You just use this command line:

```
convert -equalize input.jpg output.jpg
```

This gives you the result shown in Figure 6-14.

Figure 6-14. *The equalized version of the image in Figure 6-13*

Flipping an Image

ImageMagick refers to turning an image upside down as a *flip*. For this example, I'll show how to vertically flip the image shown in Figure 6-15.

Figure 6-15. *The original picture of a seagull*

You use this command line:

```
convert -flip input.jpg output.jpg
```

This gives you the image shown in Figure 6-16.

Figure 6-16. *The picture of a seagull, flipped vertically*

To flip the image horizontally, use the `flop` operation:

```
convert -flop input.jpg output.jpg
```

Flop acts just like flip to give you the image shown in Figure 6-17.

Figure 6-17. *The picture of a seagull, flipped horizontally*

Tinting an Image

You can also apply tint colors to images with ImageMagick. The `tint` command-line option will add the specified percentage of the current fill color to the image. Only the nonpure colors in the image will be affected; in other words, pure colors such as red and green won't change. I'll show the effects of tinting on the image shown in Figure 6-18.

Figure 6-18. *Another original picture of a flower*

If you apply a few tinting options like you did in Chapter 5, you get the set of samples shown in Figure 6-19.

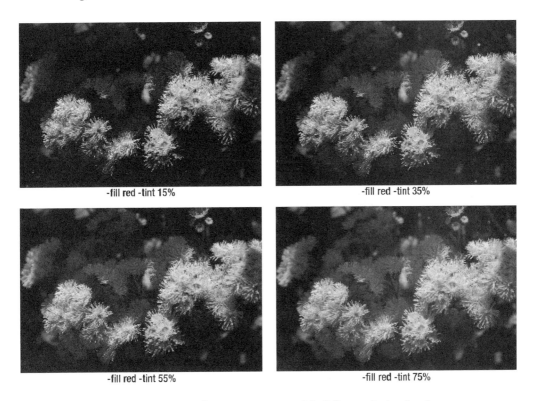

Figure 6-19. *The picture of a flower from Figure 6-18, with different tinting levels*

If you don't specify a fill color, you get the default tint of black. To apply a 10 percent tint to an image, you use a command line like this:

```
convert -fill red -tint 10% input.jpg output.jpg
```

Negating an Image

Negating a pixel is the process of inverting its value. ImageMagick can negate images with the negate command-line option. This is similar to the solarize option presented in Chapter 5 except that no threshold is applied to the decision to negate a given pixel. For this example, I'll show how to negate the picture shown in Figure 6-20.

Figure 6-20. *The original picture of some trees*

If you negate this image with this command line:

```
convert -negate input.jpg output.jpg
```

then you get the image shown in Figure 6-21.

Figure 6-21. *The picture of some trees, negated*

In contrast, the `solarize` command gives you the images shown in Figure 6-22 for varying levels of threshold.

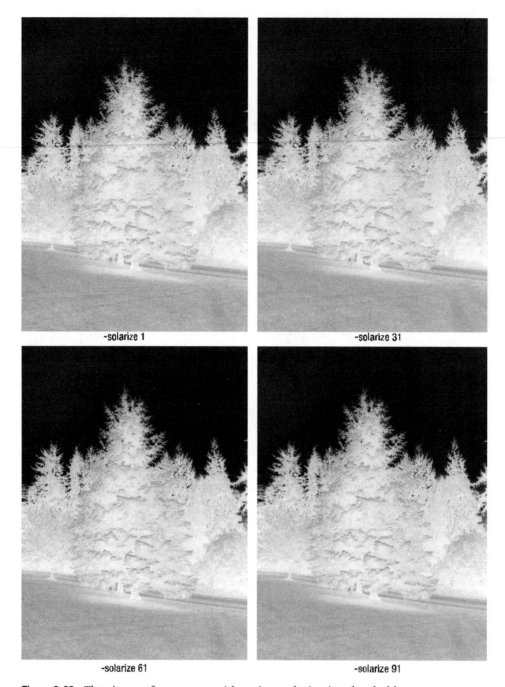

Figure 6-22. *The picture of some trees, with various solarization thresholds*

I recommend you read about solarization in Chapter 5 if you want more information.

Normalizing, Enhancing, and Modulating an Image

Normalization is the process of improving the contrast in an image so that it uses all the available color range. For example, Figure 6-23 shows a photo of Alcatraz taken through the San Francisco fog.

Figure 6-23. *Alcatraz through the fog*

Using the following command line:

```
convert -normalize input.jpg output.jpg
```

will improve the contrast in this image significantly, as shown in Figure 6-24.

Figure 6-24. *Alcatraz through the fog, after normalization*

Another way to correct contrast problems in an image is to *enhance* the photo using the `level` command-line option. This option lets you specify the black point (the color that is considered black in the image) that you'd like in the output image. You can specify this as an absolute value ranging from zero to the maximum RGB value possible in the image, but in this example I'll specify this as a percentage, because this is a more generically useful technique. To specify a black point of 20 percent of the maximum possible RGB value, use a command like this:

```
convert -level 20% input.jpg output.jpg
```

In the spirit of the examples from Chapter 5, Figure 6-25 shows a montage of some examples of various values for the black point.

Figure 6-25. *Alcatraz with varying black points specified*

You can also specify a desired white point for the image. You do this by adding another value to the specification argument. The following command specifies a white point of 50 percent of the maximum RGB value for the image, again using percentages:

```
convert -level 20%,50% input.jpg output.jpg
```

Figure 6-26 shows another montage with some various values for the white point, all using a black point of 20 percent.

Figure 6-26. *Alcatraz with a black point of 20 percent and varying white points specified*

A border has been added to these images for clarity. You can see from these examples that a white point higher than the black point produces a much nicer result. Finally, you can also specify a gamma correction value like this:

```
convert -level 20%,50%,1.0 input.jpg output.jpg
```

where the default is 1.0, which is what is specified in this example. Gamma correction is a fairly technical field that is outside the scope of this book.

Another way of tweaking the way an image looks is to modify the brightness, color saturation, and hue through *modulation*. You do this with ImageMagick with the modulate command. The following command line manipulates the brightness of an image:

```
convert -modulate 80% input.jpg output.jpg
```

This changes the brightness to 80 percent of the current brightness of the image. Figure 6-27 shows a montage of some brightness levels as examples.

Figure 6-27. *Alcatraz with varying brightness*

Let's select a brightness of 100 percent based on the images in Figure 6-27 and then modify the color saturation of the image. You do this by specifying a second part to the argument of the modulate command-line option, like this:

```
convert -modulate 100%,80% input.jpg output.jpg
```

Figure 6-28 shows some various values for the color saturation.

Figure 6-28. *Alcatraz with varying color saturations*

It's not obvious in the grayscale printing in these examples, but the first three images in Figure 6-28 are pretty much black-and-white images.

Finally, you can also adjust the hue with the modulate command, like this:

```
convert -modulate 100%,100%,80% input.jpg output.jpg
```

Figure 6-29 shows some examples of varying levels of hue.

Figure 6-29. *Alcatraz with varying levels of hue*

To make this example more obvious, Figure 6-30 shows the same operations on the normalized version of the photo.

-modulate 100%,100%,15%

-modulate 100%,100%,55%

-modulate 100%,100%,95%

-modulate 100%,100%,145%

Figure 6-30. *Alcatraz with varying levels of hue, using the normalized image*

Shearing an Image

The shear effect puts the input image at an angle. You can tilt the image horizontally and vertically in both directions (in other words, from left to right, from right to left, from top to bottom, and from bottom to top). The tilt is specified as an angle; for example, in the horizontal direction, a negative tilt is a tilt to the left, and a positive tilt is a tilt to the right. For example, to tilt an image to the right 45 degrees, you use this command line:

```
convert -shear 45 input.jpg output.jpg
```

Figure 6-31 shows some examples of shearing horizontally. In these examples I have also specified a vertical shear of zero.

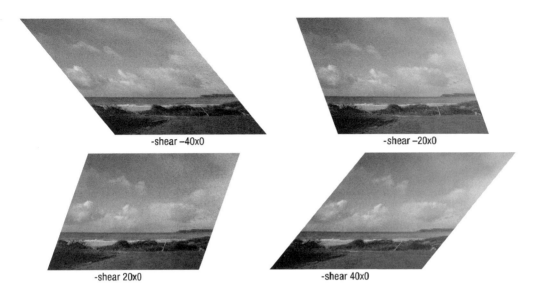

-shear −40x0

-shear −20x0

-shear 20x0

-shear 40x0

Figure 6-31. *Horizontal shearing on an image*

The empty triangles created by the shearing are filled with the color currently specified as the background color. See Chapter 7 for details on how to set the background color. You can also shear vertically by specifying a zero shear angle for the horizontal axis and then a vertical shearing. A positive angle is toward the top of the image, and a negative angle is toward the bottom. For example, to shear vertically toward the top 30 degrees, use this command line:

```
convert -shear 0x30 input.jpg output.jpg
```

Figure 6-32 shows some examples.

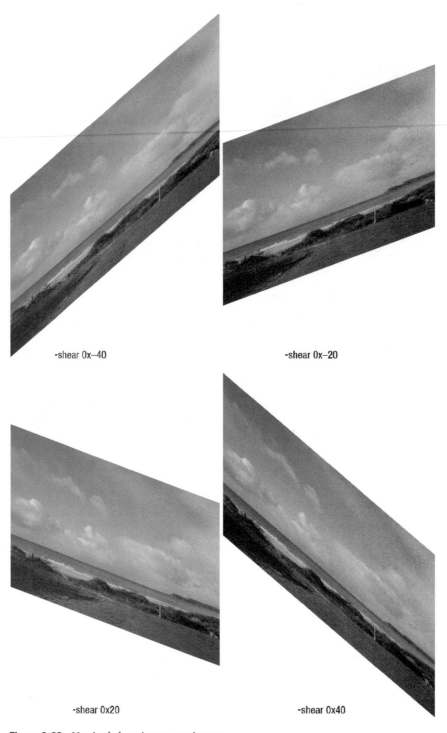

-shear 0x–40

-shear 0x–20

-shear 0x20

-shear 0x40

Figure 6-32. *Vertical shearing on an image*

You can, of course, shear in the horizontal and vertical directions at the same time. To perform the shear operation, specify the horizontal and vertical angles as arguments to the shear command-line option. For example, for a horizontal shear of 10 degrees and a vertical shear of 20 degrees, use this command line:

```
convert -shear 10x20 input.jpg output.jpg
```

Rolling an Image

The roll effect provided by ImageMagick can roll an image horizontally or vertically. A vertical roll involves taking a rectangle from the top of the image and moving it to the bottom of the image; a horizontal roll moves some of the image from the left side to the right side. You do this by specifying the horizontal roll and then the vertical roll. For example, to roll the image 100 pixels to the right and 200 pixels to the bottom, use this command line:

```
convert -roll +100+200 input.jpg output.jpg
```

This will turn the image shown in Figure 6-33 into the image shown in Figure 6-34.

Figure 6-33. *The original picture of some rainforest vegetation*

Figure 6-34. *The rolled picture of some rainforest vegetation*

To roll horizontally only, don't specify a vertical roll. To roll just vertically, specify a zero horizontal roll. To roll to the left or upward, use a negative number.

Turning Multiple Images into One Image

ImageMagick can also take groups of images and turn them into a single image. I'll cover those commands in the following sections.

Appending Images

Let's say you want to append some images together to form a strip. For example, say you have the three images shown in Figure 6-35, Figure 6-36, and Figure 6-37.

Figure 6-35. *A picture of a waterfall*

Figure 6-36. *Another picture of a waterfall*

Figure 6-37. *A third picture of a waterfall*

To append these three figures in a vertical column, you can use this ImageMagick command line:

```
convert -append input1.jpg input2.jpg input3.jpg output.jpg
```

This gives you the image shown in Figure 6-38.

Figure 6-38. *Three pictures of waterfalls, appended vertically*

To make it more obvious what is happening because of the different size of the last image, here is the same append command but with a border added:

```
convert -append input2.jpg input2.jpg input3.jpg -border 5 output.jpg
```

This gives you the image shown in Figure 6-39.

Figure 6-39. *Three pictures of waterfalls, appended vertically, with a border*

You can see in Figure 6-39 that the border will follow the edges of the images used to build the vertical column. The color used to fill in the vacant space to the right of the first two images is the background color. This is much more obvious if you set the background color to something a little more obvious than the default of white:

```
convert -background red -append input1.jpg input2.jpg input3.jpg output.jpg
```

This gives you the final vertical column shown in Figure 6-40.

Figure 6-40. *Three pictures of waterfalls, appended vertically, with a background color of red*

You can also create a horizontal row of images with the append command. To do this, just use a plus sign instead of a minus sign as the first character of the append command. For example, you can create that same column in a horizontal style:

```
convert +append input1.jpg input2.jpg input3.jpg output.jpg
```

This gives you the output shown in Figure 6-41.

Figure 6-41. *Three pictures of waterfalls, appended horizontally*

Averaging Images

ImageMagick can average pixel values and produce a new image that is this average. It does this by examining each pixel in an image, averaging that pixel's value with the corresponding pixels in the other input images, and then using that average as the value of the corresponding pixel in the output image. For this example, I'll show how to use the frames of an animation I used in the animation examples in Chapter 3. Figure 6-42 shows the individual frames of the animation.

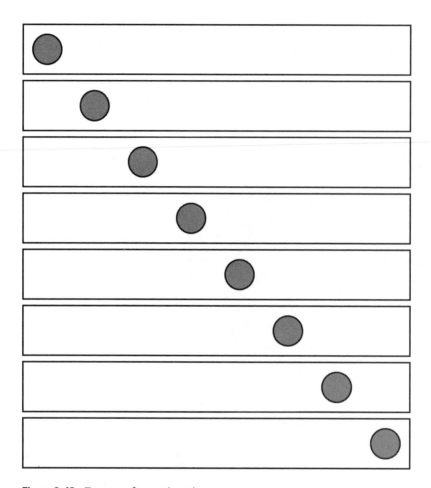

Figure 6-42. *Frames of an animation*

Now, if you average these frames with this command:

```
convert -average *.png output.png
```

you get the new image shown in Figure 6-43.

Figure 6-43. *The result of averaging the frames of an animation*

Flattening Images

Flattening refers to turning more than one image into one image by using the transparency information in the images when they're overlaid. For example, the frames in Figure 6-42 needed to be modified to make the white transparent before they can be flattened. Once the transparency information is right, you can flatten the frames with this command line:

```
convert -flatten input*.jpg output.jpg
```

This gives you the image shown in Figure 6-44.

Figure 6-44. *Frames of an animation, flattened*

You'll note that the white portion of the image hasn't been handled properly. This is because none of the images specifies the color of the inside of the rectangle. If you remove the transparency information from the first image, then you get the image shown in Figure 6-45.

Figure 6-45. *Frames of an animation, flattened, with the first frame specifying a background color for the image*

Conclusion

In this chapter, I covered all the remaining image transformations available from ImageMagick. If you combine all the preceding chapters with this one, you can see that ImageMagick can certainly do a lot for you in the imaging field. Its versatility doesn't stop there, though—you can use a number of programmatic interfaces to implement the ImageMagick functionality. The next chapter covers how to annotate existing images and create new images using the ImageMagick drawing facilities. Chapters 8 through 11 will focus on four popular programming interfaces to ImageMagick.

CHAPTER 7

■ ■ ■

Using the Drawing Commands

You can use ImageMagick to create images from scratch and annotate existing images. This chapter focuses on showing off that functionality.

Specifying Colors

Many of the drawing commands demonstrated in this chapter take an argument that is a color, so in the following three sections, I'll discuss how to specify colors for these commands. ImageMagick supports three major ways of specifying a color: named colors, HTML-style strings, and RGB tuples.

Using Named Colors

As mentioned in Chapter 1, it's possible for the administrator who set up ImageMagick to have defined a set of named colors. These names act as shortcuts to the RGB value associated with that name. The default names should still work if the administrator hasn't removed them. You can find out what named colors exist using the following command line:

```
convert -list color
```

This will list the colors that have been defined in the colors.xml file discussed in Chapter 1. Here's a sample of the list that is returned from my default installation of ImageMagick:

```
Path: /usr/lib/ImageMagick-6.2.3/config/colors.xml

Name                    Color                       Compliance
------------------------------------------------------------------------
AliceBlue               rgb(61680,63736,65535)      SVG X11 XPM
AntiqueWhite            rgb(64250,60395,55255)      SVG X11 XPM
AntiqueWhite1           rgb(65535,61423,56283)      X11
AntiqueWhite2           rgb(61166,57311,52428)      X11
AntiqueWhite3           rgb(52685,49344,45232)      X11
AntiqueWhite4           rgb(35723,33667,30840)      X11
aqua                    rgb(    0,65535,65535)      SVG
aquamarine              rgb(32639,65535,54484)      SVG X11 XPM
```

aquamarine1	rgb(32639,65535,54484)	X11
aquamarine2	rgb(30326,61166,50886)	X11
aquamarine3	rgb(26214,52685,43690)	X11
aquamarine4	rgb(17733,35723,29812)	X11
azure	rgb(61680,65535,65535)	SVG X11 XPM
azure1	rgb(61680,65535,65535)	X11
azure2	rgb(57568,61166,61166)	X11
azure3	rgb(49601,52685,52685)	X11
azure4	rgb(33667,35723,35723)	X11
beige	rgb(62965,62965,56540)	SVG X11 XPM
...		

Of course, a lot more colors exist than those defined here. (My list has 678 entries.)

Using HTML-Style Color Strings

ImageMagick also takes color arguments in the form of HTML-style color strings. For example, all the following are valid color strings:

```
#RGB                    (R,G,B are hex numbers, 4 bits each)
#RRGGBB                 (8 bits each)
#RRRGGGBBB              (12 bits each)
#RRRRGGGGBBBB           (16 bits each)
#RGBA                   (4 bits each)
#RRGGBBAA               (8 bits each)
#RRRGGGBBBAAA           (12 bits each)
#RRRRGGGGBBBBAAAA       (16 bits each)
```

To understand these values, you have to know that color is represented to ImageMagick in the form of an RGB value, which consists of red, green, and blue values. You can represent any color with an RGB value, and this is the color format used by many image formats, as well as a lot of hardware such as computer monitors. Of course, other ways of representing colors exist, such as CMYK and YUV, but given that ImageMagick uses RGB, I'll limit this discussion to the RGB values.

If, for example, you take a photo at a flower show, then you'll see the red, green, and blue values at work. Figure 7-1 shows a photo I took.

Figure 7-1. *The original picture of some flowers*

Now, if you strip out just the red, green, and blue values individually, then you get the pictures shown in Figure 7-2, Figure 7-3, and Figure 7-4.

Figure 7-2. *Just the red values for the picture of some flowers*

Figure 7-3. *Just the green values for the picture of some flowers*

Figure 7-4. *Just the blue values for the picture of some flowers*

If you group all the red values from the picture, then you can call that group the *red channel*, as discussed in Chapter 3. Figure 7-2 shows the red channel from the original photo.

Now that you've seen the color channels from a real-world photo, I'll show a slightly more contrived example, which should make this clearer. The image shown in Figure 7-5 is a simple test pattern, where the left vertical bar is a solid red, the middle vertical bar is a solid green, and the right vertical bar is a solid blue. The top horizontal bar is filled with white, and the bottom horizontal bar is filled with gray.

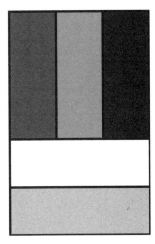

Figure 7-5. *A simple test pattern*

Figure 7-6, Figure 7-7, and Figure 7-8 show the color channels from this test pattern one at a time.

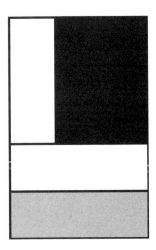

Figure 7-6. *The red channel from the test pattern*

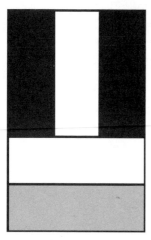

Figure 7-7. *The green channel from the test pattern*

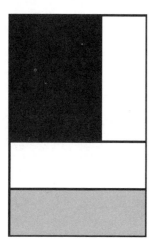

Figure 7-8. *The blue channel from the test pattern*

■Note I generated these images using ImageMagick. In Chapter 3, I introduced the gamma command-line argument. This command line allows you to set gamma correction for an image, but if you apply a gamma correction of 1.0 to the channel you want to keep and 0.0 to all the other channels, then you'll get only that one channel in the output image. For example, to extract the red channel from an image, use a gamma correction of 1.0,0.0,0.0. In addition, these images were converted to grayscale, and then normalized so that they weren't too dark for the printing process.

You can see that with the green vertical bar, for instance, the red and blue channels contribute nothing. You can also see that white consists of as much red, green, and blue as possible, and the gray bar consists of equal amounts of red, green, and blue. The darkness of the gray bar is determined by the amount of each of these three colors that is used.

Finally, it should be clear what these HTML-style color definitions are doing. Each channel is defined by a series of characters in the string, with a set of characters for each channel. You can vary the number of characters used for a channel depending on your need for accuracy, but all channels must use the same number of characters within that string. The number of characters used is also directly related to the depth of the image, which is manipulated with the depth command-line argument. (I discussed this command line in Chapter 3.)

■**Note** If you don't specify enough characters to meet the depth needs of the image, then ImageMagick adds extra characters by repetition. For example, if the red channel has only the value B specified and three characters worth of value are needed, then the value BBB will be used.

The number for a given channel is expressed as hexadecimal, which uses the letters shown in Table 7-1.

Table 7-1. *Valid Hexadecimal Values*

Hex Character	Decimal Value
0	0
1	1
2	2
3	3
4	4
5	5
6	6
7	7
8	8
9	9
A	10
B	11
C	12
D	13
E	14
F	15

So, what about the A characters mentioned in the earlier HTML color string examples? Well, one other commonly used channel, which I haven't discussed yet, is the *alpha channel*. Alpha channels are represented in HTML strings with the character *A*.

An alpha channel defines the transparency of a given pixel. For example, a pixel that has the alpha value as high as it can go for that image will be completely transparent. This is useful when you want to overlay two images and have parts of the background image still be visible. For example, say you want to lay the image shown in Figure 7-9 over the earlier example's test pattern.

Figure 7-9. *An orange donut shape*

Then you'll get the results shown in Figure 7-10.

Figure 7-10. *The donut superimposed on the test pattern*

You can see that the test pattern shows through the hole in the donut pattern. This is because the inside and outside of the donut are transparent, which means the image behind is still visible. An alpha channel is effectively a color and is handled the same way as any of the other colors; it's just not visible to the eye and has side effects when images are overlaid.

Using RGB Tuples

The final method of specifying a color is useful if you know what the decimal values for the various channels you want to set are. Two types of RGB tuples exist. To specify the RGB values, then use this form:

```
rgb(value, value, value)
```

where value is replaced by the red, green, and blue values, respectively. Alternatively, if you want to specify an alpha channel as well, then use this form:

```
rgba(value, value, value, value)
```

Specifying a Page Size

Before you can start creating images with ImageMagick, you need to know how to create an image. That's not to say you can't use these drawing commands to alter existing images—you can. However, if you want to create an image, then you need to be able to specify the size of that new image. In ImageMagick, you do this with the size command-line option. This option takes a simple geometry like many of the ImageMagick command-line options; for example, to create an image that is 100 pixels wide and 200 pixels tall, you use a size command-line option like this:

```
... -size 100x200 ...
```

This example isn't a complete command-line, however; you use it with the convert command. The convert command also expects an input image, so you use a special notation to specify an input image. This syntax allows you to tell ImageMagick what color the new image should be. For example, to create a new image that is 100 pixels wide and 200 pixels tall and is green, then you use a command line like this:

```
convert -size 100x200 xc:green output.jpg
```

The xc: syntax specifies that ImageMagick should create an image and use green as the color of that image.

Specifying a Background Color

An obvious example of a command that takes the color argument defined previously is the background color for the image. If you've been reading this book sequentially, then you've already seen the effect of setting the background color when I introduced the rotate command-line argument in Chapter 6. When you rotated the image, you automatically created four triangles in the corners of the new image, which you filled with a color using the background color option.

The command line you used at the time was as follows:

```
convert -background red -rotate 30 input.jpg output.jpg
```

which gives you the image shown in Figure 7-11.

Figure 7-11. *A picture of a flower rotated 30 degrees to the right and with the corners filled with red*

This is a good example of how to use the background command-line option. It specifies what color to use when a new background is created, for example, through rotating, shearing, and creating a new image.

Specifying the Fill Color and Stroke Color

You need to know about two other types of color when you're using ImageMagick's drawing commands. These are the *fill color*, which fills objects, and the *stroke color*, which draws the outline of objects. For example, if you draw a rectangle, then the fill color will fill the inside of the rectangle, and the stroke color will draw the outline of the rectangle.

Let's draw that rectangle:

```
convert -size 200x100 xc:lightgray -stroke green ➥
-draw "rectangle 10,10,190,90" output.jpg
```

This command line creates a light-gray image that is 200 pixels wide and 100 pixels high; it then sets the stroke color to green and draws a rectangle inset 10 pixels from all the edges of the image. This image is filled with the default fill color of black. The image is then saved to output.jpg. Figure 7-12 shows the image that this command creates.

Figure 7-12. *The rectangle you just drew*

You can also fill that rectangle with, for instance, light gray. For this command, use a white background for the image:

```
convert -size 200x100 xc:white -stroke green -fill lightgray ➥
-draw "rectangle 10,10,190,90" output.jpg
```

This gives you the image shown in Figure 7-13.

Figure 7-13. *The rectangle you just drew, filled with light gray*

You can also specify the width of the stroked line. In this example, the green line is harder to see now that the rectangle is filled. If you make the line 5 pixels wide, then you get a much more visible border around the fill color:

```
convert -size 200x100 xc:white -stroke green -strokewidth 5 ➥
-fill lightgray -draw "rectangle 10,10,190,90" output.jpg
```

This command gives you the image shown in Figure 7-14.

Figure 7-14. *The rectangle now with a 5-pixel-wide border, filled with light gray*

So, you can specify the color of the line, which is the stroke color, and the color to fill the objects you draw, which is the fill color.

Setting Gravity

ImageMagick lets you specify how some graphical operations occur using a concept called *gravity*. For instance, in Chapter 4, you saw an example that used the composite command and some corner images to create a curved corner effect on an image. The gravity command told ImageMagick which corner of the large image to place the corner images in.

Gravity is expressed in terms of a compass, as shown in Figure 7-15.

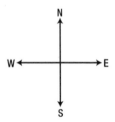

Figure 7-15. *The gravity compass*

So, the top of the image is North, and the right of the image is East. You can also specify corners with this compass, in that the top-right corner is NorthEast, for instance. To specify the center of the image, use the Center keyword. You specify the gravity on the command line with the gravity option; for example, to put a rounded corner on the top-right corner of an image, use this command:

```
composite -gravity NorthEast rounded-ne.png input.png output.png
```

Annotating an Image with Text

I'll now show how to draw by placing text on images. Remember that these images can either be new ones you created in the "Specifying a Page Size" section or be existing images. For this example, I'll use the photograph shown in Figure 7-16. Let's say you want to post this photo online.

Figure 7-16. *A photo of a building at Port Arthur in Tasmania, Australia*

You don't want people to take the image from your site, however, so perhaps you decide the best thing you can do is to put your site name on the top of the image so that people know if it's used elsewhere. You can make this annotation with this command line:

```
convert -annotate 0x0+10+10 stillhq.com input.jpg output.jpg
```

This will put the text *stillhq.com* on the image at the top-left corner and inset it 10 pixels from each edge. Note that this inset is the bottom-left corner of the first character, so you expect the text to look closer to the top of the image than it is to the left because of this. Figure 7-17 shows the result.

Figure 7-17. *The annotated photo*

Let's examine the inset a little more. If you inset by 10 pixels in each direction, you get the result shown in Figure 7-18.

stillhq.com

Figure 7-18. *The inset of the text*

Each of the gray lines in this example is 10 pixels long. Because of where the text is aligned, you end up with the top of the text being a lot closer to the top of the image compared with how close the left of the text is to the left of the image.

Now, this text isn't very visible. This is because the color choice for the text is poor, and the text really should be bigger. So, make the text bigger with the following command line:

```
convert -pointsize 24 -annotate 0x0+10+10 stillhq.com input.jpg output.jpg
```

This gives you the result shown in Figure 7-19.

Figure 7-19. *The annotated photo again, this time with bigger text*

You can see that in this example the text falls off the edge of the image, so let's shift the bottom of the text down to 30 pixels:

```
convert -pointsize 24 -annotate 0x0+10+30 stillhq.com input.jpg output.jpg
```

This gives you the result shown in Figure 7-20.

Figure 7-20. *The annotated photo again, this time with bigger text that's better aligned*

This is much nicer. Now let's change the color of the text to red, which you can do with the stroke color (as discussed in the earlier "Specifying the Fill Color and Stroke Color" section):

```
convert -pointsize 24 -stroke red -annotate 0x0+10+30 stillhq.com ➥
input.jpg output.jpg
```

This doesn't give you the result you probably expected, because the inside of the letters isn't the right color, as shown in Figure 7-21.

Figure 7-21. *The annotated photo again, with a stroke color specified*

To make this look as you expect, you need to have the inside of the letters filled with the red color as well. So, let's specify a fill color, again in the manner I demonstrated in the earlier "Specifying the Fill Color and Stroke Color" section:

```
convert -pointsize 24 -stroke red -fill red ➥
-annotate 0x0+10+30 stillhq.com input.jpg output.jpg
```

This produces the image shown in Figure 7-22.

Figure 7-22. *The annotated photo again, with a stroke and fill color specified*

This is a much nicer result in this instance. It's useful to note that the letters' fill color and stroke color don't have to be the same, which can sometimes come in handy. For completeness, it's worth noting that you can also specify the stroke width for text annotations. For example, this sets the stroke width to 3 pixels:

```
convert -pointsize 24 -stroke red -strokewidth 3 -fill red ➥
-annotate 0x0+10+30 stillhq.com input.jpg output.jpg
```

This gives you the rather indistinct version of the text shown in Figure 7-23.

Figure 7-23. *The annotated photo again, with a stroke width of 3 pixels*

You can also specify the font to use with the annotation. To do this, use the font command-line argument, which takes the name of a font as its argument. For this example, I want to use a TrueType font called Arbuckle that I downloaded from the Internet for free. The font is stored in the Arbuckle.ttf file, which means I use this command line:

```
convert -pointsize 24 -font Arbuckle.ttf -stroke red -fill red ➡
-annotate 0x0+10+30 stillhq.com input.jpg output.jpg
```

This gives you the new version of the annotation shown in Figure 7-24.

Figure 7-24. *The annotated photo with a different font selected*

WHERE DO YOU FIND FONTS?

Many Web sites make shareware and freeware fonts available for download, which is a good first place to look for fonts to use with your images. I won't recommend a specific site here, but you'll find many if you search for *free TrueType font* on Google.

You can also use the fonts installed on your system. On Microsoft Windows you'll find fonts in the `Windows/ Fonts` directory (for which the location will vary depending on your install). On Unix machines, you should check the `/usr/share` directory, which is the most likely place for fonts to be installed.

ImageMagick doesn't just support TrueType fonts, however—you can also use PostScript and OPTION1 fonts.

It's worth noting that ImageMagick has a separate specification for fixed-width fonts, which you specify in the same manner as the `font` command-line option; it's called `text-font`. You also specify another two numbers in the offset specification, which are rotation parameters.

For example, if you want to rotate in the horizontal plane, then you use the first number. Here's an annotation that has been rotated by 45 degrees:

```
convert -pointsize 24 -stroke red -fill red ➥
-annotate 45x0+10+30 stillhq.com input.jpg output.jpg
```

This gives the result shown in Figure 7-25.

Figure 7-25. *The annotated photo with a rotated annotation*

To rotate the annotation vertically, use the other number:

```
convert -pointsize 24 -stroke red -fill red ➥
-annotate 0x45+10+30 stillhq.com input.jpg output.jpg
```

This gives the result shown in Figure 7-26.

Figure 7-26. *The annotated photo with a different rotated annotation*

You can also use the gravity command-line argument to specify where on the image the text should be placed. For example, to put this text in the bottom-right corner instead of the top-left corner, then you use the gravity option like this:

```
convert -pointsize 48 -font Arbuckle.ttf -stroke red -fill red ➡
-gravity SouthEast -annotate 0x0+10+60 stillhq.com ➡
input.jpg output.jpg
```

The SouthEast argument to the gravity command-line option tells ImageMagick to put the text at the bottom-right corner of the image. You can read more about the gravity command-line option in the previous "Specifying Gravity" section. This modified command line gives you the version of the annotation shown in Figure 7-27.

Figure 7-27. *The annotated photo with the annotation in the bottom-right corner of the image*

You can also specify a box to be placed under the annotation text, which can make it a lot easier to read—in return for being more intrusive on the original image. You do this by adding the box command-line option to the command, with the argument to the box option being the color of the box. For example, the following command line adds a blue box behind the text you put on the image:

```
convert -pointsize 24 -stroke red -fill red -box blue ➥
-annotate 0x0+10+30 stillhq.com input.jpg output.jpg
```

This gives you the final image shown in Figure 7-28.

Figure 7-28. *The annotated photo with a blue box behind the text*

Finally, you can have the annotation text come from a file if you don't want to specify the text on the command line. To do this, instead of the annotation text in the command line, use an at sign and then the name of the file containing the annotation text. For example:

```
convert -annotate 0x0+10+30 @textfile.txt input.jpg output.jpg
```

Drawing Simple Shapes

ImageMagick supplies the draw command-line option to draw simple shapes. ImageMagick supports many shapes, so I'll break them down into some categories to make the explanations a little clearer. For each shape, I'll also include a simple example.

Once again, it's worth noting that all the commands demonstrated in the following sections will work on images such as photographs and diagrams, as well as these blank images that I am using here for clarity. Additionally, it's worth knowing that ImageMagick's documentation refers to these shapes as *primitives*—this is because these shapes also include other objects such as text.

Drawing a Single Point

The simplest shape is just a single pixel. For example, the following command line puts a red pixel onto a 100×100-pixel image at the point 50 pixels in from the top-left edge:

```
convert -size 100x100 -fill red -draw "point 50,50" xc:white output.png
```

This gives you the result shown in Figure 7-29. We've added a border around this image to make it a little clearer.

Figure 7-29. *A single point*

Interestingly, the point shape is drawn with the current fill color, not the current stroke color, which is something to note when you're using that shape. Setting the stroke width also has no effect on the image drawn.

Drawing a Straight Line

You can draw straight lines with the line shape. For example, the following command draws a line between 10,10 and 90,90 on another blank 100×100-pixel image:

```
convert -size 100x100 -fill red -draw "line 10,10 90,90" xc:white output.png
```

This gives you the result shown in Figure 7-30.

Figure 7-30. *A line*

Again, you can see that the fill color draws the line, not the stroke color. Note that setting the stroke width doesn't affect the image; however, the linewidth setting will change the width of the line:

```
convert -size 100x100 -stroke black -fill red -linewidth 5 ➥
-draw "line 10,10 90,90" xc:white output.png
```

This gives you the result shown in Figure 7-31.

Figure 7-31. *A thicker line*

Drawing a Rectangle

If you're reading this chapter sequentially, you already saw the rectangle command in the section "Specifying the Fill Color and Stroke Color." The rectangle shape takes two points, like the line shape, but uses those to draw a rectangle using the points as the top-left corner and the bottom-right corner. Here's an example:

```
convert -size 100x100 -stroke red -fill white -draw "rectangle 10,10 90,90"➡
xc:white output.png
```

This gives you the result shown in Figure 7-32.

Figure 7-32. *A rectangle*

You can change the size of the line used by the rectangle by using the strokewidth command-line option:

```
convert -size 100x100 -stroke red -strokewidth 5 ➡
-fill white -draw "rectangle 10,10 90,90" xc:white output.png
```

This gives you the result shown in Figure 7-33.

Figure 7-33. *A rectangle with a thicker stroke*

And finally, you can change the color with which the rectangle is filled:

```
convert -size 100x100 -stroke red -strokewidth 5 -fill lightgray ➥
-draw "rectangle 10,10 90,90" xc:white output.png
```

This gives you the result shown in Figure 7-34.

Figure 7-34. *A rectangle with a thicker stroke and filled with blue*

Drawing a Rectangle with Rounded Corners

ImageMagick can also round the corners of the rectangles that it draws. To do this, you change the name of the shape you're drawing to roundRectangle and append an extra argument to the shape description. This extra argument is the width of the circle and the height of the circle that forms those corners. For example:

```
convert -size 100x100 -stroke red -strokewidth 5 -fill lightblue ➥
-draw "roundRectangle 10,10 90,90 10,10" xc:white output.png
```

This gives you the result shown in Figure 7-35.

Figure 7-35. *A rounded rectangle with a thicker stroke and filled with blue*

This rounded rectangle has corners that are based on a circle that is 10×10 pixels. The following command tweaks that to 20×10:

```
convert -size 100x100 -stroke red -strokewidth 5 -fill lightblue ➥
-draw "roundRectangle 10,10 90,90 20,10" xc:white output.png
```

This gives you the result shown in Figure 7-36.

Figure 7-36. *A rounded rectangle with slightly different corners*

Drawing a Circle

Now I'll cover the same transformations covered with the rectangle shape in the earlier "Drawing a Rectangle" section, only this time with the circle shape. The same commands work with both rectangles and circles. For example:

```
convert -size 100x100 -stroke red -fill lightblue -draw "circle 50,50 70,70" ➥
xc:white output.png
```

The arguments to the circle shape are slightly different from the rectangle shape. The first argument is the center of the circle, and the second argument is how far the circle extends.

This gives you the result shown in Figure 7-37.

Figure 7-37. *A circle*

You can also increase the stroke width of a circle much like a rectangle:

```
convert -size 100x100 -stroke red -strokewidth 5-fill lightblue ➥
-draw "circle 50,50 70,70" xc:white output.png
```

This gives you the result shown in Figure 7-38.

Figure 7-38. *A circle with a large stroke width*

And finally, you can of course fill the circle:

```
convert -size 100x100 -stroke red -strokewidth 5 -fill red ➥
-draw "circle 50,50 70,70" xc:white output.png
```

This gives you the result shown in Figure 7-39.

Figure 7-39. *A circle with a large stroke width, filled*

Drawing an Arc

You can draw arcs with ImageMagick. You merely specify three pairs of numbers—the first two pairs of numbers are control points that dictate the size of the ellipse in which the arc is drawn. The third pair of numbers is the starting angle of the arc and the ending angle of the arc. This is a simple command-line example:

```
convert -size 100x100 -stroke red -fill lightblue -draw "arc 10,10 90,90 45,270" ➥
xc:white output.png
```

This gives you the result shown in Figure 7-40.

Figure 7-40. *An arc*

The angles for the start and end of the arc need some explanation, so refer to Figure 7-41, which will help clarify.

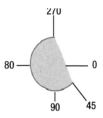

Figure 7-41. *An arc with the start and the end angles shown*

You can see on this diagram that the arc starts at 45 degrees and ends at 270 degrees.

Drawing an Ellipse

You can use a similar effect with an ellipse:

```
convert -size 100x100 -stroke red -fill lightblue -draw "ellipse 50,50 20,40 45,270" ➥
xc:white output.png
```

This gives you the result shown in Figure 7-42.

Figure 7-42. *An ellipse*

The arguments to this primitive are the center of the ellipse, the horizontal radius, and the vertical radius. The start and end angles are handled the same as in the arc primitive.

Drawing a Polyline

The polyline primitive draws lines between defined points. For example, here's a sample command line:

```
convert -size 100x100 -stroke red -fill lightgray ➥
-draw "polyline 10,10 20,40 90,90 10,90" xc:white output.png
```

This command line uses a different fill color to make the example more obvious. The command creates the image shown in Figure 7-43.

Figure 7-43. *The result of a polyline primitive*

You need a minimum of three points for this primitive.

Drawing a Polygon

The polygon primitive is the same as the polyline primitive, but the polygon finishes by returning to the starting point of the polygon:

```
convert -size 100x100 -stroke red -fill lightgray ➡
-draw "polyline 10,10 20,40 90,90 10,90" xc:white output.png
```

This gives you the result shown in Figure 7-44.

Figure 7-44. *The result of a polygon primitive*

You need a minimum of three points for this primitive.

Drawing a Bezier

The Bezier primitive draws Bezier curves. Bezier curves are based on a series of control points. The first and last points are the start and end points of the curve, and the intervening points act like gravity points and "pull" the curve toward those points. Here's an example of a Bezier curve with four control points:

```
convert -size 100x100 -stroke red -fill lightgray ➡
-draw "bezier 10,10 30,100 70,0 90,90" xc:white output.png
```

This gives you the result shown in Figure 7-45.

Figure 7-45. *The result of a Bezier primitive*

Drawing Text

You saw how to annotate text earlier in this chapter in the "Annotating an Image with Text" section. The annotate command-line option mentioned in that section is actually a shorthand method of calling the draw command-line option's text functionality, which is much the same but offers tighter control.

To annotate an image using the draw command-line option, use the text primitive, which takes a location and the string to write as arguments. For example, this command writes a word on the blank image:

```
convert -size 100x100 -stroke red -draw "text 50,50 blah" xc:white output.png
```

This gives you the result shown in Figure 7-46.

blah

Figure 7-46. *Some text created with the* draw *command-line option*

So, how do you get this extra control I promised? Well, the gravity command-line option applies to this form of text writing, much like it does for the annotate command-line option. Additionally, all the shape transformations that I'll discuss in a moment apply to the text drawn with this text primitive.

Performing Color Operations That Take a Point and a Method

The color primitive implemented by ImageMagick has a number of options that take a point and a method and then perform interesting operations with that point. For this example, I'll use the standard drawing shown in Figure 7-47.

Figure 7-47. *A sample image to which to apply point operations*

For all these operations, I'll use the point 50,50, which is in the center of the rectangle as the `point` argument.

point

The `point` argument sets the color of that single pixel with the current fill color:

```
convert -size 100x100 -stroke red -fill white -draw "rectangle 10,10 90,90" ➥
-fill black -draw "color 50,50 point" xc:white output.png
```

This gives you the result shown in Figure 7-48.

Figure 7-48. *The result of point coloring*

replace

The `replace` argument looks at the value of the pixel specified and then replaces all occurrences of that color in the image with the current fill color:

```
convert -size 100x100 -stroke red -fill white -draw "rectangle 10,10 90,90" ➥
-fill black -draw "color 50,50 replace" xc:white output.png
```

This gives you the result shown in Figure 7-49.

Figure 7-49. *The result of replace coloring*

floodfill

The floodfill argument fills the inside of the shape that contains the specified point with the current fill color:

```
convert -size 100x100 -stroke red -fill white -draw "rectangle 10,10 90,90" ➥
-fill black -draw "color 50,50 floodfill" xc:white output.png
```

This gives you the result shown in Figure 7-50.

Figure 7-50. *The result of floodfill coloring*

filltoborder

The filltoborder argument is similar to the floodfill option, but replaces the border as well:

```
convert -size 100x100 -stroke red -fill white -draw "rectangle 10,10 90,90" ➥
-fill black -draw "color 50,50 filltoborder" xc:white output.png
```

As this command sets the entire image to black, I haven't included an example of it's output.

reset

The reset argument colors all pixels anew:

```
convert -size 100x100 -stroke red -fill white -draw "rectangle 10,10 90,90" ➥
-fill black -draw "color 50,50 filltoborder" xc:white output.png
```

Similar to filltoborder, this command sets the entire image to black, so I haven't included an example of it's output.

Transforming Your Drawings

The draw command-line option supports a number of transformations that you can apply to the primitives you use. In this series of examples, I'll show how to use the draw command-line option to put some primitives on top of an existing image and then use the transformation's primitives to rearrange the elements I'm drawing. I'll put them on top of the image shown in Figure 7-51 to show that the draw transformations don't affect that image.

Figure 7-51. *The original water image*

This command line draws a simple stick-figure man and some text:

```
convert -fill blue -font mailrays.ttf -pointsize 96 ➡
-draw "circle 100,100 125,125 rectangle 65,150 135,300 ➡
text 200,300 Water" input.jpg output.jpg
```

This gives you the final image shown in Figure 7-52 to use for comparisons. (I'm sorry I'm not more artistic!)

Figure 7-52. *The water image, with a drawing over the top*

Rotating the Drawing

The first transformation I'll apply is the rotate transformation primitive. The rotate command-line option takes an argument that is the number of degrees to rotate clockwise, much like the rotate command-line option discussed in Chapter 6. Here's an example:

```
convert -fill blue -font mailrays.ttf -pointsize 96 ➥
-draw "rotate -15 circle 100,100 125,125 rectangle 65,150 135,300 ➥
text 200,300 Water" input.jpg output.jpg
```

This rotates all the drawn elements but not the original picture, as shown in Figure 7-53.

Figure 7-53. *The water image, with a drawing over the top that is rotated by -15 degrees*

You can choose to rotate only some of the drawn elements by changing where you place the rotate command:

```
convert -fill blue -font mailrays.ttf -pointsize 96 ➥
-draw "circle 100,100 125,125 rectangle 65,150 135,300 rotate -15 ➥
text 200,300 Water" input.jpg output.jpg
```

This will rotate only the text, as shown in Figure 7-54.

Figure 7-54. *The water image, with just the text rotated*

Translating a Drawing

You can also translate a drawing. Translation is the process of shifting a drawing by a given amount, for example, 40 pixels to the left or 150 pixels down. The following command translates the drawing used in the previous example down 150 pixels:

```
convert -fill blue -font mailrays.ttf -pointsize 96 ➥
-draw "translate 0,150 circle 100,100 125,125 rectangle 65,150 135,300 ➥
text 200,300 Water" input.jpg output.jpg
```

This gives you the result shown in Figure 7-55.

Figure 7-55. *The water image, with the drawing shifted down*

Scaling a Drawing

Perhaps you're really happy with the drawing you've done but now realize that it's the wrong size and want to scale the whole drawing without changing all those coordinates. You just provide a scale primitive with the horizontal scaling factor and vertical scaling factor. For example, the following command makes the drawing one-and-a-half times its current width but half its current height:

```
convert -fill blue -font mailrays.ttf -pointsize 96 ➡
-draw "scale 1.5,0.5 circle 100,100 125,125 rectangle 65,150 135,300 ➡
text 200,300 Water" input.jpg output.jpg
```

This gives you the result shown in Figure 7-56.

Figure 7-56. *The water image, with the drawing scaled horizontally and vertically*

Skewing a Drawing

Finally, for the transformations you can apply to your drawing, you can skew the drawing. You can perform this skew either horizontally or vertically by using different commands. For example, to skew horizontally, simply specify the number of degrees to skew with the skewx primitive:

```
convert -fill blue -font mailrays.ttf -pointsize 96 ➥
-draw "skewx 30 circle 100,100 125,125 rectangle 65,150 135,300 ➥
text 200,300 Water" input.jpg output.jpg
```

This gives you the result shown in Figure 7-57.

Figure 7-57. *The water image, with a horizontal skew*

You can also skew vertically with the skewy primitive:

```
convert -fill blue -font mailrays.ttf -pointsize 96 ➥
-draw "skewy 30 circle 100,100 125,125 rectangle 65,150 135,300 ➥
text 200,300 Water" input.jpg output.jpg
```

This gives you the result shown in Figure 7-58.

Figure 7-58. *The water image, with a vertical skew*

Combining Transformation Primitives

Of course, you can combine transformations; for example, to rotate just the word *water* but move the whole drawing down 150 pixels, use a command line like this:

```
convert -fill blue -font mailrays.ttf -pointsize 96 ➥
-draw "translate 0,150 circle 100,100 125,125 rectangle 65,150 135,300 ➥
rotate -15 text 200,300 Water" input.jpg output.jpg
```

This gives you the result shown in Figure 7-59.

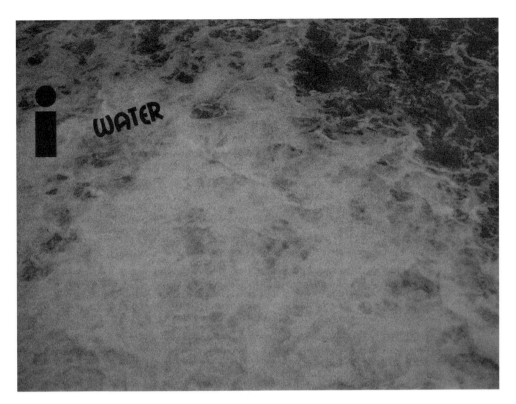

Figure 7-59. *Drawing on the water image and combining a translation and rotation*

Using More Than One Draw Command

Nothing is stopping you from using more than one invocation of the draw command-line option. In fact, this is sometimes required—for instance, if you want to change the color you're filling shapes with, you'll have to use more than one command. The following command keeps the stick-figure man blue but makes the text red:

```
convert -fill blue -font mailrays.ttf -pointsize 96 ➥
-draw "circle 100,100 125,125 rectangle 65,150 135,300" -fill red ➥
-draw "text 200,300 Water" input.jpg output.jpg
```

This gives you the result shown in Figure 7-60.

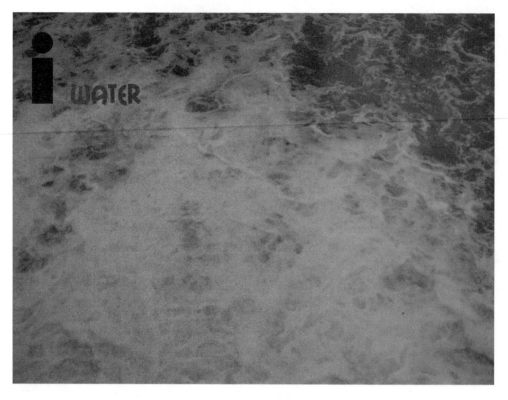

Figure 7-60. *The water image, using two* draw *commands*

Compositing Images with the draw Command

As discussed in Chapter 4, you can use the composite command to combine images. You can achieve a simple equivalent with the convert command's draw command-line option. For example, to place an image over another, you can use syntax like this:

```
convert -draw "image Over 100,100 418,222 fern.png" input.jpg output.jpg
```

For this example, input.jpg looks like the image shown in Figure 7-61.

Figure 7-61. *A photo of a fern*

And fern.png looks like the image shown in Figure 7-62.

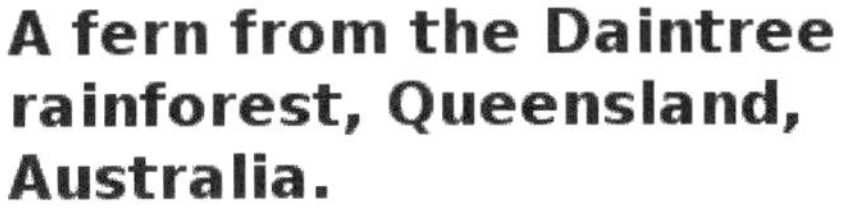

A fern from the Daintree rainforest, Queensland, Australia.

Figure 7-62. *A label to apply to the fern image*

This will result in an output image that looks like Figure 7-63.

Figure 7-63. *A labeled fern image*

The first pair of numbers in the command line is the inset to start the image at, and the second pair of numbers is the size of the image. If you use 0,0, then the real size of the image is used; any other pair of numbers will result in the image being scaled to the specified size. You don't just need to place images over one another, however. The following sections highlight the available operators and show examples of their effects.

Using the Over Operator

This is the transformation used previously, so I won't include an example here. It's listed here for completeness.

Using the In Operator

The In operator replaces the image data under the overlay image with the overlay image. None of the image data from the original image in the covered area is used, even if the overlay image specifies transparency:

```
convert -draw "image In 100,100 418,222 fern.png" input.jpg output.jpg
```

This gives you the result shown in Figure 7-64.

Figure 7-64. *A labeled fern image, using* In

Using the Out Operator

The Out operator removes the section of the input image that would be covered by the overlay image but doesn't actually put the overlay image into that space:

```
convert -draw "image Out 100,100 418,222 fern.png" input.jpg output.jpg
```

This gives you the result shown in Figure 7-65.

Figure 7-65. *A labeled fern image, using* Out

Using the Atop Operator

The Atop operator produces something visually the same as the Over operator, except in the case where the overlay image falls outside the input image's original boundary. For example, here's the Atop operator with the coordinates tweaked so that the image does fall outside the edge of the input image:

```
convert -draw "image Atop 500,300 418,222 fern.png" input.jpg output.jpg
```

This gives you the result shown in Figure 7-66.

Figure 7-66. *A labeled fern image, using* Atop

In previous releases of ImageMagick, the Over operator would have extended the image to include all of the overlay image. This is no longer the case, however.

Using the Xor Operator

The Xor operation will apply the exclusive "or" Boolean operator to the input image and the overlay image and then place the result into the output image. The exclusive "or" operator is often known as the *logical difference*, because it's a simple bit difference operator. If the value of two Bits from the input images is different, then the value of the exclusive or operation is a 1. Otherwise, the value of the exclusive or is 0. This command line:

```
convert -draw "image Xor 100,100 418,222 fern.png" input.jpg output.jpg
```

gives you the results shown in Figure 7-67.

Figure 7-67. *A labeled fern image, using* Xor

Using the Plus Operator

The Plus operator adds the existing pixel value in the input image to the pixel value of the overlay image and then uses that new value in the output image. If the new pixel value is higher than can be stored in the output image, it's truncated to the maximum possible value for that image. The matte channel value is set to opaque. For example:

```
convert -draw "image Plus 100,100 418,222 fern.png" input.jpg output.jpg
```

This gives you the result shown in Figure 7-68.

Figure 7-68. *A labeled fern image, using* Plus

Using the Minus Operator

Minus does the same as the Plus operator, except that the base image's pixel value is subtracted from the overlay image's pixel value. If the new value is less than zero, then it's made zero. The matte channel value is set to opaque. For example:

```
convert -draw "image Minus 100,100 418,222 fern.png" input.jpg output.jpg
```

This gives you the result shown in Figure 7-69.

Figure 7-69. *A labeled fern image, using* Minus

Figure 7-69 is too dark to show well in printed form, but if you look closely, you can see an outline of the letters in the image.

Using the Difference Operator

Difference is similar to the Minus operator, except that an absolute value is applied to the result of the subtraction, so the new pixel value doesn't need to be forced to not be negative. For example:

```
convert -draw "image Difference 100,100 418,222 fern.png" input.jpg output.jpg
```

This gives you the result shown in Figure 7-70.

Figure 7-70. *A labeled fern image, using* Difference

Again, the image doesn't show up well after the printing process has done its thing; but again, if you look closely, you can see the outline of the letters. The ImageMagick documentation suggests that the Difference operator is useful to see differences in similar images. You can test this by reusing the images I demonstrated the compare command with in Chapter 4.

Figure 7-71 shows the starting image.

Figure 7-71. *The original image*

Figure 7-72 shows the image after it has been changed by the spread transformation discussed in Chapter 5, with a spread factor of 1.

Figure 7-72. *The image after a spread factor of 1*

The compare command, which specializes in noting differences in images, produces the image shown in Figure 7-73.

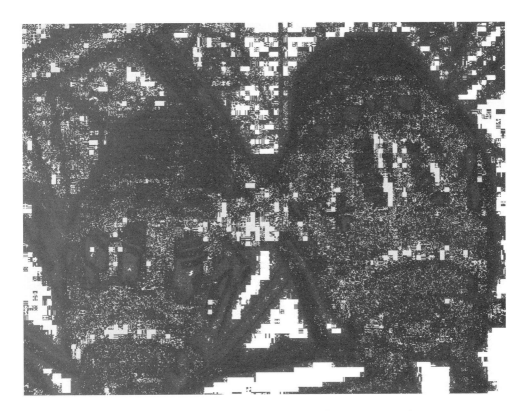

Figure 7-73. *The output of the compare command run on the two previous images*

And the Difference operator produces the image shown in Figure 7-74.

Figure 7-74. *The output of the* Difference *operator on the two images*

You can see that the claim from the ImageMagick documentation is correct, at least for this set of input images. In fact, the Difference output is actually more useful in this case than the output of the compare command.

Using the Multiply Operator

Multiply multiplies the pixel value from the input image with the pixel value from the overlay image to determine the value of the pixel in the output image:

```
convert -draw "image Multiply 100,100 418,222 fern.png" input.jpg output.jpg
```

This gives you the result shown in Figure 7-75.

Figure 7-75. *A labeled fern image, using* Multiply

You can also use the Multiply operator to create drop shadows.

Using the Bumpmap Operator

The Bumpmap operator takes the input image and shades it with the overlay image:

```
convert -draw "image Bumpmap 100,100 418,222 fern.png" input.jpg output.jpg
```

This gives you the result shown in Figure 7-76.

Figure 7-76. *A labeled fern image, using Bumpmap*

Performing Other Tasks with These Composition Operators

You can also use these composition operators with the composite command:

```
composite -compose In fern.png input.jpg output.jpg
```

This gives you a similar result to the earlier In example, as shown in Figure 7-77.

Figure 7-77. *Using the* In *composition operator with the* composite *command*

The difference here is that the scaling of the overlay image and the inset of the overlay image haven't been specified.

Antialiasing Your Images

When I introduced rasters in Chapter 2, I discussed pixels. When you draw a straight line, you can imagine that the process involves turning on pixels along the path of the line to make the line appear on the image. It turns out it's more complicated than that, though, because what if a pixel should be half on? In a simple black-and-white image where you don't have any options, you simply ignore that pixel and move on, which results in a jagged image. The alternative that is available in images with more possible color levels is that you can half turn on the pixel by making only that pixel half as bright. This is called *antialiasing*.

I'll now show an example. Figure 7-78 shows some text drawn with ImageMagick.

Figure 7-78. *The word* magick

If you zoom in on this image, you can see these half-turned-on pixels, as shown in Figure 7-79.

Figure 7-79. *Zooming in on the word* magick

The gray pixels around the edge of the letters are antialiasing at work. Now, Figure 7-80 shows that text without antialiasing.

Figure 7-80. *The word* magick, *without antialiasing*

You can see already that the text doesn't look as good. Now let's zoom in again, as shown in Figure 7-81.

Figure 7-81. *The word magick, without antialiasing, zoomed in*

You can see that the version without antialiasing looks more jagged.

Sometimes you don't want antialiasing, however. For example, on LCD monitors, antialiased text often looks fuzzy and slightly out of focus. ImageMagick therefore lets you turn antialiasing on and off. To use antialiasing, which is the default, just use the antialias command-line option. Here's how to create the earlier antialiased example:

```
convert -antialias -font captains.ttf -pointsize 140 -size 300x120 ➥
-fill black -annotate 0,0+10+100 "Magick" xc:white output.png
```

To disable antialiasing, use the +antialias command-line option, like this:

```
convert +antialias -font captains.ttf -pointsize 140 -size 300x120 ➥
-fill black -annotate 0,0+10+100 "Magick" xc:white output.png
```

Framing an Image

ImageMagick can place frames around images, which is something I briefly touched upon in Chapter 2 when I showed how to remove frames with the trim command-line option. The way you create one of these frames with ImageMagick is with the frame command-line option. At its most basic, the command takes the thickness of the frame horizontally and vertically as its arguments, like this:

```
convert -frame 10x10 input.jpg output.jpg
```

The first number is the amount to add to each side of the image, and the other number is the amount to add to the top and the bottom of the image. This gives you the output shown in Figure 7-82.

Figure 7-82. *A photo with a frame*

Now, this gray frame isn't very visible here, so I've opted to create a dark green frame using the mattecolor option:

```
convert -mattecolor darkgreen -frame 10x10 input.jpg output.jpg
```

This gives you a dark green frame; Figure 7-83 shows the result.

Figure 7-83. *A photo with a dark green frame*

You can specify two other arguments with the frame command-line option. These are the outer bevel width and the inner bevel width. Here's an example of setting the outer bevel width to 5 and the inner bevel width to 0:

```
convert -mattecolor darkgreen -frame 10x10+5+0 input.jpg output.jpg
```

This gives you the result shown in Figure 7-84.

Figure 7-84. *A photo with a dark green frame and an outer bevel*

You can also set the inner bevel:

```
convert -mattecolor darkgreen -frame 10x10+0+5 input.jpg output.jpg
```

This gives you the result shown in Figure 7-85.

Figure 7-85. *A photo with a dark green frame and an inner bevel*

Finally, you can set both and outer and an inner bevel:

```
convert -mattecolor darkgreen -frame 10x10+5+5 input.jpg output.jpg
```

This gives you the result shown in Figure 7-86.

Figure 7-86. *A photo with a dark green frame and an outer and an inner bevel*

Writing Each Step of the Way

ImageMagick lets you save the intermediate state of images. For example, if you reuse the drawing example from earlier in this chapter but split the draw command into more than one draw command, it looks like this:

```
convert -fill blue -font mailrays.ttf -pointsize 96 ➥
-draw "circle 100,100 125,125 rectangle 65,150 135,300" -fill red ➥
-draw "text 200,300 Water" -spread 2 input.jpg output.jpg
```

This gives you the result shown in Figure 7-87.

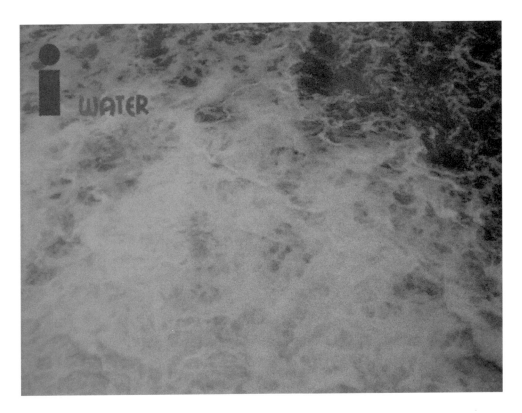

Figure 7-87. *A sample image*

You can see the various stages the image goes through by changing this command line to use the `write` command-line option to save intermediate stages of the image. For example, here's a new command line that uses the `write` command-line option:

```
convert input.jpg -fill blue -font mailrays.ttf -pointsize 96 ➥
-draw "circle 100,100 125,125 rectangle 65,150 135,300" -write stage1.jpg ➥
-fill red -draw "text 200,300 Water" -write stage2.jpg -spread 2 output.jpg
```

This gives you two intermediate images, which look like Figure 7-88 and Figure 7-89.

Figure 7-88. *The first intermediate image*

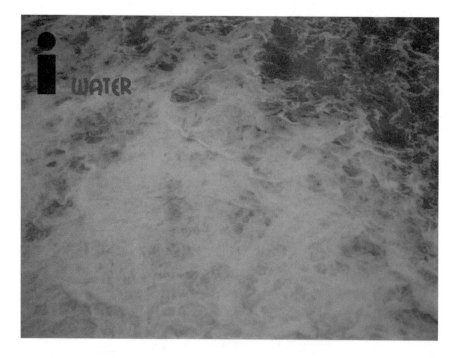

Figure 7-89. *The second intermediate image*

Notice with this command line that I have moved the input image to much earlier in the command line; this is because without this, ImageMagick will store a list of the operations to perform and then execute them when it sees the name of the input filename; as a result, the intermediate images would be the same as the output image because they no longer are spread between the image-changing operations.

Applying Affine Matrices

You can apply matrices to your images to produce image effects such as translations and shearing. To explain what is happening here, I'll briefly introduce some matrix manipulations on images. This is the identity matrix:

$$\begin{bmatrix} 1 & 0 & 0 \\ 0 & 1 & 0 \\ 0 & 0 & 1 \end{bmatrix}$$

This matrix, if applied to an image, will result in the same image coming out the other end. To pass a matrix to ImageMagick, you use the `affine` command-line option and pass it six values, which look like this:

$$\begin{bmatrix} sx & rx & 0 \\ ry & sy & 0 \\ tx & ty & 1 \end{bmatrix}$$

The last column is constant, so it isn't passed to ImageMagick. The values are passed in this order: `sx`, `rx`, `ry`, `sy`, `tx`, `ty`. For example, to pass the identify matrix, you pass this:

```
convert -affine 1,0,0,1,0,0 -transform input.jpg output.jpg
```

The `transform` command-line option tells ImageMagick to apply the current affine matrix to the image. Figure 7-90 shows the input image.

Figure 7-90. *An image to which to apply affine matrix transformations*

The result of applying the identity matrix is the same image you started with, so I won't include the image twice.

You can see that the identity matrix doesn't change the image. To translate images, you use the last two values in the affine matrix specification. For example, to shift the image 50 pixels horizontally and 100 pixels vertically, you use this matrix:

$$\begin{bmatrix} 1 & 0 & 0 \\ 0 & 1 & 0 \\ 50 & 100 & 1 \end{bmatrix}$$

This results in the following command line:

```
convert -affine 1,0,0,1,50,100 -transform input.jpg output.jpg
```

This gives you the translated image that's shown in Figure 7-91. (I've applied a frame to the image to make the output a little clearer.)

Figure 7-91. *After the application of a translation*

Note that the size of the image hasn't changed except that the image has been shifted down. You can scale images as well; for example, if you halve everything in the horizontal plane and multiply everything in the vertical plane by 1.5, you require a matrix like this:

$$\begin{bmatrix} 0.5 & 0 & 0 \\ 0 & 1.5 & 0 \\ 0 & 0 & 1 \end{bmatrix}$$

This gives you the following command line:

```
convert -affine 0.5,0,0,1.5,0,0 -transform input.jpg output.jpg
```

This produces the scaled image shown in Figure 7-92.

Figure 7-92. *After the application of scaling*

This transformation does change the size of the image.

You can also apply a shear with a simple matrix. For example, to shear by half the size of the image vertically, you use this matrix:

$$\begin{bmatrix} 1 & 0.5 & 0 \\ 0 & 1 & 0 \\ 0 & 0 & 1 \end{bmatrix}$$

This gives you the following command line:

```
convert -affine 1,0.5,0,1,0,0 -transform input.jpg output.jpg
```

This produces the sheared image shown in Figure 7-93.

Figure 7-93. *After the application of a vertical shearing*

Similarly, to shear horizontally by half the size of the image, you use a matrix like this:

$$\begin{bmatrix} 1 & 0 & 0 \\ 0.5 & 1 & 0 \\ 0 & 0 & 1 \end{bmatrix}$$

This gives you the following command line:

```
convert -affine 1,0,0.5,1,0,0 -transform input.jpg output.jpg
```

This produces the sheared image shown in Figure 7-94.

Figure 7-94. *After the application of a horizontal shearing*

You can also rotate the image by a given angle with a matrix like this:

$$\begin{bmatrix} \text{cosine(angle)} & \text{sine(angle)} & 0 \\ -\text{sine(angle)} & \text{cosine(angle)} & 0 \\ 0 & 0 & 1 \end{bmatrix}$$

For example, to rotate an image by 15 degrees, use this matrix:

$$\begin{bmatrix} 0.9659 & 0.2588 & 0 \\ -0.2588 & 0.9659 & 0 \\ 0 & 0 & 1 \end{bmatrix}$$

This gives you this command line:

```
convert -affine 0.9659,0.2588,-0.2588,0.9659,0,0 -transform input.jpg output.jpg
```

This produces the rotated image shown in Figure 7-95.

Figure 7-95. *After the application of a rotation*

You can also combine operations in one of these matrices. For instance, you'll notice that the rotated image doesn't all fall onto the canvas anymore. You can translate the image back onto the canvas by moving it 250 pixels horizontally, which, when combined with the rotation, produces a matrix like this:

$$\begin{bmatrix} 0.9659 & 0.2588 & 0 \\ -0.2588 & 0.9659 & 0 \\ 250 & 0 & 1 \end{bmatrix}$$

This gives you the following command line:

```
convert -affine 0.9659,0.2588,-0.2588,0.9659,250,0 -transform input.jpg output.jpg
```

This produces the rotated image shown in Figure 7-96.

Figure 7-96. *After the application of a rotation and translation*

Conclusion

This is the last chapter in this book that deals with the ImageMagick command line, and you've come a long way throughout these seven chapters. In this chapter, I discussed the various ImageMagick drawing commands, which let you modify existing images and create new images. ImageMagick can perform a lot of cool operations on images from the command line, and I hope you've enjoyed the last seven chapters. They should form a useful reference for your future use of the command-line tools.

The next four chapters focus on examples of programmer interfaces to ImageMagick, so you'll need to know something about coding to get much utility from those chapters. If you're a programmer, you'll get to see how to use different aspects of ImageMagick in Perl, C, Ruby, and PHP. Finally, I'll finish off the book with a chapter on where to go from what's covered in this book.

## CHAPTER 8

PerlMagick: ImageMagick Programming with Perl

This chapter introduces how to use ImageMagick with the Perl programming language. It's not a Perl programming tutorial, however, so you'll need to look elsewhere if you're not familiar with the Perl programming language. Later chapters in this book cover other programming languages (although each of them deals with a different example); therefore, if your interest lies with another language, then refer to those chapters.

I've called the code presented in this chapter `photomagick`.

Presenting the Problem

This chapter discusses an online photo management system that uses PerlMagick. When my first child was born, I rushed out and bought a digital camera with the intention of taking as many pictures as I could. I ended up being a little too successful, however, and soon had an unmanageably large collection of pictures to manage and post online. This chapter will show how to use an online photo management system to solve this sort of problem. This system manages the photos from digital cameras (and presumably scanned pictures) from the initial categorization to the publication of selected pictures on the Internet in various sizes with various metadata. This publication engine can also plug into simple content management systems (CMSs), such as the Blosxom blog engine that I use for http://www.stilllhq.com. The code I'll present in this chapter is a basic system, and it's entirely possible you'll want to modify the code to meet your needs, which is why the code is licensed under the GNU General Public License (GPL) and is available online at http://www.stilllhq.com/imagemagick/perl/photomagick/.

The foundation of a system such as this is the manner in which the metadata about the pictures is stored. In this case, I've chosen to use flat text files, which are stored in the same directory as the images, for a few reasons. This matches what I was already doing, it makes it easy to back up the metadata with the images themselves, it's much easier to set up initially for new users, and the advantages of a database are minimized because I'm not talking about massive amounts of metadata.

The code in this chapter generates static HTML files and versions of images on disk. This is so that the Web server doesn't have to cope with the extra load of generating the pages. Disk space is cheap, and I've found recently that, as the popularity of my site increases, avoiding dynamic generation (especially with images) is a good idea.

I'll now discuss the format for the metadata file. There is one file per directory of images named META (in all capitals), which has the following format:

```
dsc_0443.jpg    none            mikal
dsc_0444.jpg    none            mikal
dsc_0445.jpg    none    right   mikal
dsc_0446.jpg    diary           taffy_cat
dsc_0447.jpg    diary           taffy_cat
dsc_0448.jpg    diary           taffy_cat
dsc_0449.jpg    diary           taffy_cat
```

The format for the file is relatively simple, as you can see. The file contains four columns. The first is the name of the image file, and the second is where the image is to be placed on the Web server (none means the image isn't public). The third is whether the image needs to be rotated; you can see that one of the images here needs to be rotated to the right. The fourth column is a series of keywords for the image, with an underscore between the keywords. These keywords are packed into the image filename when it's posted online, which helps services such as Google's image search find them during crawls. Each of these columns is delimited with tab characters.

If an image is found that doesn't have an entry, then the system attempts to use JPEG EXIF tags to extract the value for rotation or just applies a reasonable default (no rotation, publication, or keywords).

For the moment, this code assumes that all the images you're publishing are JPEG images (that is, have a filename that ends in .jpg). There's no real reason for this limitation other than it works for the images I'm currently using. Removing this limitation is left as an exercise for you.

Introducing the Format for This Chapter

In this chapter, I'll present the code for the system and then discuss what is happening where relevant. I don't expect you to type this code manually, which is the reason for the annotated style of inclusion here. If you want to run this code, then download it from http://www.stillhq.com/imagemagick/perl/photomagick/. After discussing the code, I'll walk you through how to use it.

Introducing the Code Structure

The code for PhotoMagick.pm is a Perl module containing common routines shared between the CGI script and the command-line publication tool. Also, a CGI script presents the user interface for photomagick. This script is called photomagick. Finally, a command-line tool takes the metadata entered in photomagick and creates the output HTML files. This command is called pmpublish.

Using PhotoMagick.pm

The shared module is PhotoMagick.pm. The case for the filename is inconsistent from the rest of the scripts so that the naming convention is the same as other Perl modules. Here's the code for the module:

```perl
package PhotoMagick;

use strict;
use Class::Struct;

# There is one of these for each image or for each image in the META file
struct( metaitem => [
    target  => '$',
    rotate => '$',
    rotatedesc => '$',
    keywords => '$',
]);
```

This structure is used to pass around the parsed metadata from the file format described previously. This is so I can build an array of these structures and keep the data together for ease of handling.

```perl
# This function reads the META file and returns the parsed metadata as a
# hash reference.
#
# Pass in the path to the directory containing the META file.
sub readmeta{
    my($path) = @_;
    my($META, $meta, $temp);

    open META, "< $path/META" or return undef;
    while(<META>){
        if(/^([^\t]*)\t([^\t]*)\t([^\t]*)\t([^\t]*)$/){
            my $mi = new metaitem;
            $mi->target($2);

            if(($3 eq "none") || ($3 eq "")){
                $mi->rotate("no");
            }
            else{
                $mi->rotate($3);
            }
            $mi->keywords($4);
            $meta->{$1} = $mi;
            }
        else{
            print STDERR "Poorly formatted META line: $_\n";
            }
        }
    close META;

    return $meta;
}
```

The previous function parses the META file (if one exists) and returns the array of structures mentioned previously. It works by reading each line of the file and using a regular expression to split the line up into the fields that are expected. These are then stored in a new structure, which is added to the array that is eventually returned.

```perl
# This function reads the META target file and returns the parsed metadata
# as a hash reference. The format is simple -- the first line is the title,
# and everything else is the description
#
# Pass in the path to the META target file
sub readmetatarget{
    my($path) = @_;
    my($META, $meta);

    open META, "< $path" or return undef;
    while(<META>){
        if($meta->{'title'} eq ""){
            $meta->{'title'} = $_;
        }
        else{
            $meta->{'description'} = $meta->{'description'}.$_;
        }
    }
    close META;

    return $meta;
}
```

Similarly, this function reads the metadata associated with a specific target for this directory of images. This information is returned in a simple hash:

```perl
1;
```

The trailing 1 in this file is an artifact of Perl modules and tells Perl that the module loaded correctly.

Introducing photomagick

In this section, I'll show you the CGI script that is used to present the user interface for the system. I don't claim to be a user interface design expert, and this code is mainly about demonstrating the functionality of PerlMagick, so don't pay too much attention to how the HTML looks.

```perl
#!/usr/bin/perl

use strict;
use CGI;
use CGI::Carp qw(fatalsToBrowser);
use File::Find;
use Image::Magick;
use Image::EXIF;

use PhotoMagick;
```

The first task the script does is load the dependencies for the script. This includes the Perl CGI module, a helper for returning error messages to the user inside the browser when die() is called, a module for helping find files in the file system, the PerlMagick module (which is called Image::Magick), and a helper for reading EXIF information from the JPEG images.

Why do you use a helper for the EXIF information? Well, ImageMagick is entirely capable of reading this information from the file but is too slow to work with this application. In some of my testing, I was publishing sets of images that had 300 to 400 images each. ImageMagick took so long reading the EXIF information that the browser would time out before the page could be sent to the browser.

When I get to the EXIF reading in the code later in this section, I'll show you how to use ImageMagick instead, in case you want to do that. Next in the code is the configuration information:

```perl
#######################
# Configuration options

# The directory the images are in
my($directory) = "/data/pictures";

# The HTML header for the top of the page
my($header) = "<html><head><title>photomagick</title></head><body>";

# This is the tick image used for the published column
my($tick) = "<img src=\"http://www.stillhq.com/common/tick.png\">";

# The HTML footer for the bottom of the page
my($footer) = "</body></html>";

# This is a comma-separated list of the targets that users should be allowed
# to set for an image. This must contain an entry named none
my(@targets) = split(/,/, "andrew,matthew,events,diary,none");
```

Both this script and pmpublish have configuration needs, which are included in this format at the start of the file. If you want to use photomagick, then you'll need to change these configuration options to match your system. Table 8-1 describes the configuration options.

Table 8-1. *Configuration Options for* photomagick

Option	Explanation
directory	The directory that contains the directories of images.
header	A simple HTML header to display at the top of the user interface. Use this to customize the look of photomagick.
footer	Similarly, some HTML to append to the HTML generated by photomagick.
targets	A Perl array of the possible targets for images when published. Images can be in one of several targets, including the special case none, which means no publication.

This is how the target concept works: All the output of the pmpublish command will be placed into the output path specified in that script. Inside this output path, you'll find a number of target directories. Inside these target directories can be another optional part element, which is also discussed in a moment. Finally, a directory with the same name as the input directory is created, and the images and HTML files are placed there. Figure 8-1 shows what happens.

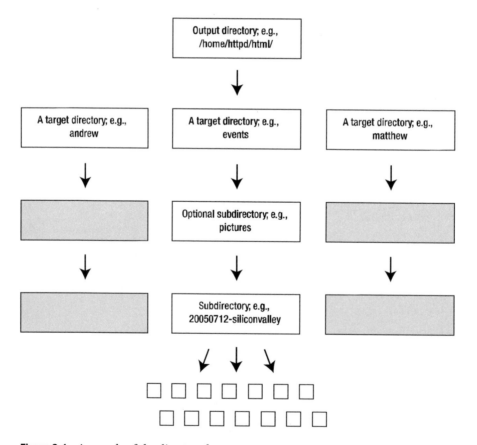

Figure 8-1. *A sample of the directory layout*

In this example, images published to the events target will end up in
/home/httpd/html/events/pictures/20050712-siliconvalley.

Let's return to the photomagick CGI script. The following describes the flow for the CGI
script:

```
#######################

# This is the CGI context
my($result);

# The logic for the CGI script is as follows:
#    A user enters with no arguments to the CGI script. They get a list of
#    the image directories, the number of images within the directory, and
#    information about whether the images have been published. They select a
#    directory.
#
#    If a directory is specified, then the user is asked to enter metadata
#    for each of the pictures. Some JavaScript helpers make this
#    more fun.
#
#    If a directory is specified and there is an action=commit, then the
#    metadata is committed and the images are moved to their destination,
#    with any conversion that might be needed.
#
#    If a directory is specified and there is an action=image, then the
#    full-sized image is returned. This needs the filename for the image to
#    be provided as well. This command also supports a rotate option as well.
#
#    If a directory is specified and there is an action=thumbnail, then a
#    small-sized image is returned. This needs the filename for the image to
#    be provided as well. This command also supports a rotate command.
```

If no arguments are specified, then a list of directories is displayed. The user selects one of
these directories, and a page of thumbnails and metadata is displayed. The user enters details
and then submits the Web form. Next, the metadata is saved to the META file.

```
$result = new CGI();

# Almost all pages have a header
if(($result->param('action') ne "image") &&
   ($result->param('action') ne "thumbnail")){
   print $result->header;
   print "$header\n\n";
```

```
    # All pages except the top need a return to the top link
    if($result->param('dir') ne ""){
        my($url) = $result->self_url(-full);
        $url =~ s/\?.*$//;

        print "<a href=\"".$url.
            "\">Return to the directory list</a><br/><br/>\n";
    }
}
```

Almost all the pages have an HTML header; this eliminates repetitive code. The only requests that don't have this HTML header are those that return images, where the header is handled in the code for that actual request. This standard HTML header includes a link to return users to the top-level page where they can select a different directory.

The code for each of the different pages that CGI uses is reversed here, with the logically last used page first and the first page used last. This is to make the flow of the if statements more logical.

```
if($result->param('action') eq "commit"){
    # We're committing the changes to the metadata file and rearranging
    # images
    my($filename, $target);
    my($dir) = $result->param('dir');
    my($inputpath) = "$directory/$dir";
    my($META);

    print "Processing images...\n";
    open META, "> $inputpath/META" or
        die "Couldn't open the META file for output";

    # Write out the meta file for the images
    print "<ul>\n";
    foreach $filename (split(/,/, $result->param('images'))){
        print META "$filename\t".
            $result->param("$filename-target")."\t".
            $result->param("$filename-rotate")."\t".
            $result->param("$filename-keywords")."\n";
        print "<li>$filename</td>\n";
    }
    close META;

    foreach $target (@targets){
        if($result->param("$target-title") ne ""){
            open META, "> $inputpath/META-$target" or
                die "Couldn't open the META-$target file for output";
```

```
            print META $result->param("$target-title")."\n";
            print META $result->param("$target-description")."\n";
            close META;
        }
    }

    print "</ul><br/><br/>\n";
    print "You now need to run the pmpublish command to generate the HTML\n";
    print "$footer";
}
```

The commit action takes the metadata entered earlier and writes it to the META file in the directory with all the images. An additional file per target contains a simple description of the images placed in that target. For example, if the images from a given run are put into the events and diary targets, then the files META-events and META-diary will also exist. These extra files create the CMS entries when pmpublish is run.

```
elsif(($result->param('action') eq "image") &&
      ($result->param('dir') ne "") &&
      ($result->param('filename') ne "")){
    # This will convert the output image to JPEG if needed
    my($dir, $filename, $rc);

    $dir = $result->param('dir');
    $filename = $result->param('filename');

    my($image);
    $image = new Image::Magick;
    print "Content-Type: ".$image->MagickToMime('jpg')."\n\n";

    $rc = $image->Read("$directory/$dir/$filename");
    die "$rc" if $rc;

    if($result->param('rotate') ne ""){
        $rc = $image->Rotate($result->param('rotate'));
            die "$rc" if $rc;
    }

    binmode STDOUT;
    $rc = $image->Write('jpg:-');
    die "$rc" if $rc;
}
```

The image action returns a copy of the image that is passed in the HTTP request. This is invoked by clicking a thumbnail image in the metadata entry form. The image path is expressed as the filename and a directory name. The image is read from disk using ImageMagick, and then it's returned via standard out so that the image is sent via the CGI interface correctly. This is the first example in the code of ImageMagick being used, so it's worth paying attention to this action.

The PerlMagick module is initialized by this line:

```
$image = new Image::Magick;
```

This sets up the image variable for PerlMagick use. The script then asks ImageMagick what the MIME type for the file type "jpg" is. The MIME type is needed because this action constructs its own HTTP response header so that it can return the image on standard out later.

Then the image is read into a variable using the PerlMagick Read() method. The image is written back out using the PerlMagick Write() method. The filename passed to Read() is where to read the image from, and the filename passed to Write() is where to write the image. The first part of the output filename is a format specifier, and the hyphen after the colon tells ImageMagick to write the image to standard out. Additionally, the image is rotated if needed, based on the rotate argument to the HTTP request. The Rotate() method takes the number of degrees to rotate the image by, just like the rotate command-line option to convert.

The return code of any of these PerlMagick operations determines whether the method failed. This is why the value is put into the variable rc and then checked with a die() statement. This action returns the image full size, so this is all that it needs to do. The thumbnail action, which I'll discuss next, also resizes the image.

```perl
elsif(($result->param('action') eq "thumbnail") &&
      ($result->param('dir') ne "") &&
      ($result->param('filename') ne "")){
    # This assumes that the image being returned is a JPEG file
    my($dir, $filename, $rc);

    $dir = $result->param('dir');
    $filename = $result->param('filename');

    # Produce a thumbnail of the image on the fly
    my($image);
    $image = new Image::Magick;
    print "Content-Type: ".$image->MagickToMime('jpg')."\n\n";

    $rc = $image->Read("$directory/$dir/$filename");
    die "$rc" if $rc;

    $rc = $image->Thumbnail(geometry=>$result->param('xsize').'x'.
                                      $result->param('ysize'));
    die "$rc" if $rc;

    if($result->param('rotate') ne ""){
        $rc = $image->Rotate($result->param('rotate'));
            die "$rc" if $rc;
    }
```

```
    binmode STDOUT;
    $rc = $image->Write('jpg:-');
    die "$rc" if $rc;
}
```

The thumbnail action is the same as the image action, except that the image is also resized to the desired thumbnail size. This action inserts the thumbnails onto the main metadata entry form by using a standard HTML IMG tag and including the CGI script as the location of the image. The image can then be generated on the fly using PerlMagick. I use the ImageMagick Thumbnail() operation to reduce the size of the image, because it discards the image metadata, which isn't needed in a thumbnail.

The size of the thumbnail is configurable and was entered by the user on the same form that they selected a directory to publish. Allowing the user to set the size of the thumbnail makes publishing a large number of images on a large monitor easier, as you can make the thumbnails bigger, which in turn makes deciding which ones to publish easier.

```
elsif($result->param('dir') ne ""){
    # The user has specified a directory
    my($rowalt, $meta, $filename, $temp);
    $rowalt = 1;

    javascript();
    print "<table width=\"100%\">\n";
    print $result->start_form(-name=>'metadata');
    print $result->hidden('action', 'commit');
    print $result->hidden('dir', $result->param('dir'));

    $temp = "$directory/".$result->param('dir');
```

This is the metadata form, which has been referred to a few times so far. If a directory has been specified and none of the previous actions was executed, then this action will occur. The metadata form is a simple HTML form, which includes clickable thumbnails of all the images, as well as some JavaScript helpers to make data entry easier.

```
$meta = combine($temp, PhotoMagick::readmeta($temp), getimages($temp));
```

photomagick gathers metadata from two places. First, the readmeta() method from the PhotoMagick module is called, which reads the META file from the image directory. This file should contain keywords and so forth for the images, although it's entirely possible that images are missing from the META file; in fact, if the directory has never been published before, it will be empty.

Additionally, getimages() returns a list of all the images in the directory. Both of these lists are passed into combine(), which returns one coherent list of images with all the metadata known about them. I'll discuss combine() when its code comes up later in this section.

```
$temp = "";
foreach $filename(sort(keys(%$meta))){
    $temp = "$temp$filename,";
}
    print $result->hidden('images', $temp);
```

A hidden HTML form element lists all the images on the form. This is needed so that the commit action knows which images need metadata saved to the META file.

```perl
foreach $filename(sort(keys(%$meta))){
    print "<tr";
    if($rowalt == 1){ print " bgcolor=\"CCCCCC\""; $rowalt = 0; }
    else{ $rowalt = 1; }
    print ">";

    # Name anchor for linking, image and link to full-sized image
    print "<td valign=\"top\"><a name=\"$filename\">";
    print "<div align=\"center\">";
    print "<a href=\"".$result->self_url.
        ";action=image".
        ";filename=$filename";
    if($meta->{$filename}->rotate eq "right"){
        print ";rotate=90";
    }
    elsif($meta->{$filename}->rotate eq "left"){
        print ";rotate=-90";
    }
    print "\">";

    print "<img src=\"".$result->self_url.
        ";action=thumbnail".
        ";filename=$filename;";
    if($meta->{$filename}->rotate eq "right"){
        print ";rotate=90";
    }
    elsif($meta->{$filename}->rotate eq "left"){
        print ";rotate=-90";
    }
    print "\">";
    print "</a></div></td>\n";

    # The option to enter simple metadata for the image
    print "<td valign=\"top\">Target:<br/><ul>";
    print $result->radio_group(-name=>"$filename-target",
                                    -values=>[@targets],
                                    -default=>$meta->{$filename}
                                        ->target,
                                    -linebreak=>'true');
    print "</ul>";
    $result->autoEscape(0);
    print $result->button(-name=>"$filename-filldown",
                                -value=>'Fill this target down',
                                -onClick=>"flowdown('$filename-target',
                                                'radio');");
```

```perl
$result->autoEscape(1);
print "</td>\n";

print "<td valign=\"top\">Rotation:<br/><ul>";
print $result->radio_group(-name=>"$filename-rotate",
                                     -values=>['left', 'no', 'right'],
                                     -default=>$meta->{$filename}
                                            ->rotate,
                                     -linebreak=>'true');
print "</ul>";
print "<i>".$meta->{$filename}->rotatedesc."</i>";
print "</td>";

print "<td valign=\"top\">";
$temp = $meta->{$filename}->keywords;
$temp =~ s/_/ /g;
print "<div align=\"center\">";
print $result->textarea(-name=>"$filename-keywords",
                                     -rows=>5, -cols=>"80",
                                     -default=>$temp);
print "<br/>";
$result->autoEscape(0);
print $result->button(-name=>"$filename-filldown",
                                -value=>'Fill this description down',
                                -onClick=>"flowdown('$filename-keywords',
                                                    'textarea');");

$result->autoEscape(1);

print "</td></tr>\n";
}
```

Each image gets a row in the table, with an alternating background to make the list more readable. This row includes a thumbnail, radio buttons to select a target, radio buttons to select a rotation for the image, and a text edit area to define keywords for the image.

```perl
print "</table>\n";
print $result->hidden(-name=>"js-end");

# Ask for a description of each target
my($target);
foreach $target (sort(@targets)){
    print "<br/><br/>\n";
    print "Enter a description of the images published in $target:<br/>\n";
    print "<ul>Title: ";
    print $result->textfield(-name=>"$target-title",
                                    -size=>"80");
    print "<br/>";
```

```perl
        print $result->textarea(-name=>"$target-description",
                                        -rows=>"8", -cols=>"100");
        print "</ul>";
    }


    print "<br/><br/><div align=\"center\">";
    print $result->submit('submit', ' Commit changes ');
    print "</div>";
    print $result->end_form;
    print "$footer";
    print "\n\n";
}
```

Additionally, each of the possible targets has a description field, which is populated with a default if a description has previously been specified.

```perl
else{
    # Output a list of the directories
    my($dir, $rowalt);
    $rowalt = 1;

    print $result->start_form(-name=>'dirselect');
    print "Specify a thumbnail size, or use the default:\n";
    print "<ul>";
    print "<table>\n";
    print "<tr><td>Horizontal size:</td><td>".
        $result->textfield(-name=>'xsize', -size=>5, -value=>'128')."</td></tr>";
    print "<tr><td>Vertical size:</td><td>".
        $result->textfield(-name=>'ysize', -size=>5, -value=>'96')."</td></tr>";
    print "</table>\n";
    print "<i>These sizes are for unrotated images, and will be flipped for ➥
rotated images\n";
    print "</ul><br/><br/>\n";
```

The final action is the one that is performed if no arguments are specified. This is intended to be a list of the directories that the user can select to publish. First the script outputs a simple form to let the user select the thumbnail size to use for the metadata page.

```perl
    print "<table width=\"100%\">\n";
    print "<tr><td>Directory</td>";
    print "<td width=\"10%\">Number of images</td>";
    print "<td width=\"10%\">Published</td></tr>\n";

    foreach $dir (sort(getdirectories($directory))){
        # We want only the part of the directory after the path, as
        # using the rest on the URL would be an information leak
        $dir =~ s/$directory\///;
```

```
        print "<tr";
        if($rowalt == 1){ print " bgcolor=\"CCCCCC\""; $rowalt = 0; }
        else{ $rowalt = 1; }
        print ">";

        # The edit button
        print "<td>".$result->submit('dir', $dir);

        # Number of images
        print "<td>".getimages("$directory/$dir")."</td>";

        # Published?
        print "<td>";
        if(ispublished("$directory/$dir")){ print "$tick"; }
        else{ print " "; }
        print "</td>";

        print "</tr>\n";
    }
    print "</table>";
    print $result->end_form;
    print "$footer";
    print "\n\n";
}
```

A row is output, again with alternating background color, for each directory that is found in the pictures directory that contains at least one image.

```
####################################

# This function combines the read metadata with the actual list of images.
# There are three possible cases. An image that actually exists is listed
# in the META file, the image is listed in the meta file and doesn't exist, or
# the image exists but doesn't have an entry in the META file. This function
# handles all three of these cases and produces a hash of all the images
# that need processing.
#
# Pass in the output of the readmeta function and the getimages function,
# in that order.
sub combine{
    my($path, $meta, @images) = @_;
    my($image, $combinedmeta, $exifreader, $orient, $data);
```

As the comment mentions, the purpose of this function is to ensure that all images end up in the hash. You do this by combining what the META file gave you with a complete list of images in the directory. If an image is found that isn't mentioned in the META file, then it will be added to the hash with a reasonable default. This method also has the side effect of dropping images that are listed in the META file but don't exist on disk.

```
foreach $image (@images){
    if(exists($meta->{$image})){
        $combinedmeta->{$image} = $meta->{$image};
    }
    else{
        print STDERR "Reading EXIF information for $image\n";
        $combinedmeta->{$image} = new metaitem;

        # Infer orientation from JPEG EXIF data. We have to unload
        # the EXIF reader so it works next time.
        $exifreader = new Image::EXIF("$path/$image") or
            die "No EXIF read";
        $data = $exifreader->get_all_info() or
            die "EXIF read failed";
        undef($exifreader);

        #print STDERR Dumper($data)."\n";

        $orient = $data->{image}->{'Image Orientation'};
        print STDERR "$orient\n";
```

The EXIF extraction uses the EXIF helper as discussed previously. If you want to do the same thing with ImageMagick, then you just use the Get method on the image. For example, to get the model information for the camera used, you use this code:

```
my($exif_model) = $image->Get('%[EXIF:Model]');
```

This is, however, much slower. Let's return to the script:

```
        if($orient eq "Right-Hand, Top"){
            $combinedmeta->{$image}->rotate("right");
        }
        elsif($orient eq "Left-Hand, Bottom"){
            $combinedmeta->{$image}->rotate("left");
        }
        else{
            # Top-left
            $combinedmeta->{$image}->rotate("no");
        }
        $combinedmeta->{$image}->target("none");

        $combinedmeta->{$image}->rotatedesc($orient);
    }
}

return $combinedmeta;
}
```

```perl
# Call this function to get back a list of the images in a given directory.
# This makes the assumption that there are no subdirectories. It would be
# easy to support that, though.
#
# Pass in the path to the directory that contains the images.
sub getimages{
    my($path) = @_;
    my(@images);

    print STDERR "Finding images in $path\n";
    find(sub{
            # Modify the next line to support file formats other than JPEG
            # if needed
            if($File::Find::name =~ /\/([^\/]*\.jpg)$/i){
                push(@images, $1);
            }
    }, $path);

    return @images;
}
```

As discussed in its opening comment, the previous function gets a list of images from a directory. It's important to note that this includes all images in subdirectories as well. The follow option on the File::Find invocation allows Perl to follow symbolic links.

```perl
# This function is similar to the above but returns a list of the
# directories containing at least one image.
#
# Pass in the path to the parent directory
sub getdirectories{
    my($path) = @_;
    my(%directories);

    find({
        wanted=>sub{
        # Again, this needs to be tweaked if other image formats are
        # to be supported
            if($File::Find::name =~ /\/([^\/]*\.jpg)$/i){
                # This is a horrible, horrible hack
                $directories{$File::Find::dir} = "yes";
            }
        },
        follow=>1
    },
    $path);

    return keys %directories;
}
```

Similarly, this previous function returns a list of the directories containing images.

```perl
# Determine whether a directory has been published on the Web
#
# Returns true if the directory has been published
sub ispublished{
    my($path) = @_;

    return( -f "$path/META" );
}
```

The previous function is a really simple one to determine whether images have been published. It does this just by defining published as the existence of a META file in that directory. Next there is a JavaScript helper function:

```perl
# Output the JavaScript for the description page
sub javascript{
    print <<EOF;
<script language="JavaScript">
<!--
function flowdown ( startid, type ){
  found = false;
  descr = "NOTSET";

  for (var i = 0; i < document.metadata.elements.length; i++) {
    if(document.metadata.elements[i].name == "js-end") {
      found = false;
    }

    if(document.metadata.elements[i].type == type) {
      if(document.metadata.elements[i].name == startid) {
        found = true;
      }

      if(found) {
        if(descr == "NOTSET") {
          if(type == "radio") {
            if(document.metadata.elements[i].checked == true) {
              descr = document.metadata.elements[i].value;
            }
          }
          else {
            descr = document.metadata.elements[i].value;
          }
        }
```

```
      if(type == "radio") {
        if(document.metadata.elements[i].value == descr) {
          document.metadata.elements[i].checked = true;
        }
      }
      else {
        document.metadata.elements[i].value = descr;
      }
    }
  }
 }
}

// -->
</script>
EOF
}
```

The last function in the CGI script is a simple one that outputs the JavaScript for the metadata entry interface. This implements a simple flow-down of either the target or the description of an image.

Introducing pmpublish

The pmpublish command takes the metadata saved into the META file by the CGI script and turns that into a set of HTML pages and images ready for your Web site. The pmpublish command is separate from the photomagick CGI script because publishing all the images can take a little while, depending on the number and size of the images involved. Additionally, it makes it easier to republish images later, such as if the templates you use for your site change.

```
#!/usr/bin/perl

# This script takes a directory name on the command line and uses the META
# files in that directory to publish nice HTML

use strict;
use File::Copy;
use File::Copy::Recursive;
use Image::Magick;
use Image::EXIF;
use PhotoMagick;
```

```
#######################
# Configuration options

# The output configuration
my($outdirectory) = "/data/stillhq.com/html";
my($indexdirectory) = "/home/mikal/blog";
my($subdirectory) = "pictures";
my($baseurl) = "http://www.stillhq.com/";
```

These configuration options change where the output files are placed, where the index file for the published images (the CMS entry) is put, any subdirectory as discussed for the images inside the target directory, and the base URL for the Web site the images are being published on—in other words, the name of the server on which the images are being published.

```
# The name of the main index file
my($indexfilename) = "000001.blog";
my($indexfileitems) = 20;
```

These configuration options affect the index file. The first is the name of the file, which in my case needs to conform to the naming convention implemented by the blog engine I use for http://www.stillhq.com. If you're just generating HTML, then this would be something like index.html. The other option is the number of thumbnails to include in the index file before appending the "more thumbnails" link that points to a page with all the thumbnails on it.

```
# Configuration for template files
my($templatepath) = "/data/pictures/photomagick";
my($imageindextemplate) = "$templatepath/image.html";
my($indextemplate) = "$templatepath/index.blog";
my($thumbnailtemplate) = "$templatepath/thumbnails.html";
```

These configuration options are the name and location of the three template files—the index template, the thumbnails template, and the image template. All these files are stored in the template path directory in this example.

```
# Configuration options for the image annotation
my($logofont) = "$templatepath/schmotto.ttf";
my($logosize) = 60;
my($logocolor) = "white";
my($logotext) = "stillhq.com";
my($logogravity) = "SouthWest";
```

This final set of configuration options defines the font, size, color, text, and location of an annotation to place on the images on the site to stop them being misused. In my case, I stamp images on my site with the text *stillhq.com*.

```
#######################
# Variables

my($meta, $filename, $image, $rc);
my($target,$targetpath, $targetindexpath, $targeturl);
my($keywords, $temp, $template);
```

```perl
my(%imagecount, %imagethumbnails, %allimagethumbnails);
my($INDEX);

# We need to have the final directory name for the output path
my($dir) = $ARGV[0];
$dir =~ s/^.*\/([^\/])/$1/;
print "Processing $dir...\n";

# Read in the META file
$meta = PhotoMagick::readmeta($ARGV[0]);

# Load in the image template file
$template = readfile("$imageindextemplate");

# Make STDOUT unbuffered
{
    my $ofh = select STDOUT;
    $| = 1;
    select $ofh;
}
```

Whilst not related to ImageMagick, it's interesting to note that this is the Perl way of turning off buffering of standard output. This happens so that progress information is displayed to the user without Perl waiting for an end of line to display the text.

```perl
# Process the images
foreach $filename(sort(keys(%$meta))){
    $target = $meta->{$filename}->target;

    # Work out where this images is going, and ensure that directory exists
    $targetpath = "$outdirectory/$target/$subdirectory/$dir";
    $targetindexpath = "$indexdirectory/$target/$subdirectory/$dir";
    $targeturl = "$baseurl$target/$subdirectory/$dir";

    # If this is a new target for this directory name, then we need to create
    # the start of the index file in that directory
    if($target ne "none"){
        File::Copy::Recursive::pathmk($targetpath);
        File::Copy::Recursive::pathmk($targetindexpath);
        print "\t$filename: [target is $target] ";

        # Turn spaces in the keywords into underscores
        $keywords = $meta->{$filename}->keywords;
        $keywords =~ s/ /_/g;
        chomp($keywords);
```

```
# Open the image
$image = new Image::Magick();
$rc = $image->Read("$ARGV[0]/$filename");
die "$rc" if $rc;
```

This is another example of ImageMagick reading in a file from disk. It's followed by similar rotation and resizing code to that which you have seen already.

```
# If the image needs to be rotated, then now is the time to do it
if($meta->{$filename}->rotate eq "right"){
    print "[rotating right] ";
    $rc = $image->Rotate('90');
    die "$rc" if $rc;
}
elsif($meta->{$filename}->rotate eq "left"){
    print "[rotating left] ";
    $rc = $image->Rotate('-90');
    die "$rc" if $rc;
}


# Resize the image: large sized is currently 1280x960
if($meta->{$filename}->rotate eq "no"){
    $rc = $image->Sample(geometry=>'1280x960');
}
else{
    $rc = $image->Sample(geometry=>'960x1280');
}
die "$rc" if $rc;


# Place a logo on the bottom of the large image
$rc = $image->Annotate(font=>$logofont,
                                pointsize=>$logosize,
                                fill=>$logocolor,
                                text=>$logotext,
                                gravity=>$logogravity);
die "$rc" if $rc;
```

This code annotates the image with the annotation preferences specified in the configuration.

```
# Write out the large size
$rc = $image->Write("$targetpath$keywords-$filename");
die "$rc" if $rc;
print "large ";


# Medium-sized
if($meta->{$filename}->rotate eq "no"){
    $rc = $image->Sample(geometry=>'x480');
}
```

```perl
else{
    $rc = $image->Sample(geometry=>'x640');
}
die "$rc" if $rc;
$rc = $image->Write("$targetpath$keywords-medium-$filename");
die "$rc" if $rc;
print "medium ";

# Small-sized. Vertically aligned images will come out smaller so
# that they all line up on the thumbnails page
$rc = $image->Sample(geometry=>'x96');
die "$rc" if $rc;
$rc = $image->Write("$targetpath$keywords-small-$filename");
die "$rc" if $rc;
print "small ";

# The thumbnail in the index file for this image
if($imagecount{$target} eq ""){
    $imagecount{$target} = 1;
}

# Only some appear on the CMS index page
if($imagecount{$target} < $indexfileitems + 1){
    $imagethumbnails{$target} = $imagethumbnails{$target}.
        "<a href=\"$targeturl"."image".$imagecount{$target}.".html\">".
        "<img src=\"$targeturl$keywords-small-$filename\"></a> \n\n";
}
elsif($imagecount{$target} == $indexfileitems + 1){
    $imagethumbnails{$target} = $imagethumbnails{$target}.
        "<br/><br/><a href=\"$targeturl"."thumbnails.html\">".
        "See more thumbnails</a>";
}

# All of them appear on the thumbnails page, though
$allimagethumbnails{$target} = $allimagethumbnails{$target}.
    "<a href=\"$targeturl"."image".$imagecount{$target}.".html\">".
    "<img src=\"$targeturl$keywords-small-$filename\"></a> \n\n";
print "index ";
```

This code handles the thumbnails being in the right place. You do this by building up a string of the HTML for the thumbnails for the index page and another string containing the HTML for the thumbnails for the thumbnail page.

```perl
# The index file for this image
my($url) = "/$target/$subdirectory/$dir"."image".
    $imagecount{$target}.".html";
my($parenturl) = "/$target/$subdirectory/$dir";
my($largeimage) = "/$target/$subdirectory/$dir/$keywords-$filename";
```

```perl
my($mediumimage) = "/$target/$subdirectory/$dir/$keywords-medium-$filename";
my($smallimage) = "/$target/$subdirectory/$dir/$keywords-small-$filename";
my($thumbnailspage) = "/$target/$subdirectory/$dir"."thumbnails.html";

my($exifreader, $data);
$exifreader = new Image::EXIF("$ARGV[0]/$filename") or
    die "No EXIF read";
$data = $exifreader->get_all_info() or
    die "EXIF read failed";
undef($exifreader);

my($exif_model) = $data->{camera}->{'Camera Model'};
my($exif_datetime) = $data->{other}->{'Image Digitized'};
my($exif_exposuretime) = $data->{image}->{'Exposure Time'};
my($exif_fnumber) = $data->{image}->{'F-Number'};
my($exif_isospeed) = $data->{image}->{'ISO Speed Rating'};
my($exif_shutterspeed) = $data->{image}->{'Shutter Speed'};
my($exif_exposurebias) = $data->{image}->{'Exposure Bias'};
my($exif_aperture) = $data->{image}->{'Lens Aperture'};
my($exif_meteringmode) = $data->{image}->{'Metering Mode'};
my($exif_flash) = $data->{image}->{'Flash'};
my($exif_focallength) = $data->{image}->{'Focal Length]'};

# Remove those pesky underscores from the keywords again
$keywords =~ s/_/ /g;
```

All of the previous code is devoted to setting up the substitution variables for the image template. This includes getting the keywords into the right form and extracting metadata about the image from the EXIF tags in the JPEG file.

```perl
# Write out the image template
$temp = $template;
$temp =~ s/(\$\w+(?:::)?\w*)/"defined $1 ? $1 : ''"/gee;

open INDEX, "> $targetpath"."image".
    $imagecount{$target}.".html" or
    die "Couldn't open image detail page";
print INDEX $temp;
close INDEX;
print "html ";
```

The template is then written out to disk. See the "Using the Templates" section for more information about the template language.

```perl
    $imagecount{$target}++;
}
else{
    print "\t$filename: [target is $target] ";
}
```

```perl
    print "\n";
}


# Now output the index pages based on their templates
foreach $target (keys(%imagethumbnails)){
    if($target ne "none"){
        my($title, $description, $thumbnails);

        $targetpath = "$outdirectory/$target/$subdirectory/$dir";
        $targetindexpath = "$indexdirectory/$target/$subdirectory/$dir";

        $template = readfile("$indextemplate");
        my($targetdesc) = PhotoMagick::readmetatarget("$ARGV[0]/META-$target");
        $title = $targetdesc->{'title'};
        $description = $targetdesc->{'description'};
        $thumbnails = $imagethumbnails{$target};

        $template =~ s/(\$\w+(?:::)?\w*)/"defined $1 ? $1 : ''"/gee;

        open INDEX, "> $targetindexpath/$indexfilename" or
            die "Could open index file";
        print INDEX $template;
        close INDEX;
        print "CMS entry: $targetindexpath$indexfilename\n";

        # And the thumbnail page
        $template = readfile("$thumbnailtemplate");
        $thumbnails = $allimagethumbnails{$target};
        my($url) = "/$target/$subdirectory/$dir"."thumbnails.html";
        my($parenturl) = "/$target/$subdirectory/$dir";


        $template =~ s/(\$\w+(?:::)?\w*)/"defined $1 ? $1 : ''"/gee;

        open INDEX, "> $targetpath/thumbnails.html" or
            die "Could open index file";
        print INDEX $template;
        close INDEX;
        print "Thumbnails: $targetpath"."thumbnails.html\n";
    }
}


print "Processing finished\n\n";
```

Similarly, the previous code handles writing out the index and thumbnail templates for the directory. The basic technique is the same as for the image template.

```
# Read the named file into a string
#
# Takes the filename
sub readfile{
    my($filename) = @_;
    my($INDEX, $retval);

    $retval = "";
    open INDEX, "< $filename" or die "Couldn't open $filename";
    while(<INDEX>){
        $retval = "$retval$_";
    }
    close INDEX;

    return $retval;
}
```

The previous function reads an entire file into a string. This reads in the templates so they can be processed as a string earlier in the code.

Using the Templates

photomagick has three templates—the index template is the template used for the index to the images; the thumbnail template is the template used to display all the thumbnails, because you can limit the number that appear on the index page; and finally, the image template is used once for each image and displays information from the EXIF tags stored in the JPEG file.

The template language is simple; each template variable is in the following form:

```
$description
```

where $ indicates a variable, in this case one named description. The following sections explain each of the templates in turn.

Using the Index Template

The index template is the simplest, especially for the CMS engine I use; this is the entire template:

```
$title
$description

<br/><br/>

$thumbnails

[btags: photo]
[icbm: home]
```

The CMS engine treats the first line as the page title and then everything else as the body of the blog post, so this template just appends the thumbnails to the end of the blog post and then handles blog search engine tagging. The valid variables for this template are as follows:

- `title`: The title of the page as entered on the metadata page

- `description`: The description of the page as entered on the metadata page

- `thumbnails`: The thumbnails to display on the index page

Using the Image Template

The image template is a little more complex, as it's HTML in my setup. (It's possible that it is another CMS page in your environment.) Remember that it's possible for any of these templates to produce whatever format you want, as long as it's a file on disk at the end. Because of its complexity, I won't include a sample here. The variables possible for the template are as follows:

- `url`: The absolute URL for this image page, not including the domain name

- `parenturl`: The absolute URL for the directory containing this image file and the images themselves, not including the domain name

- `largeimage`: The URL for the large image, not including the domain name

- `mediumimage`: The URL for the medium image, not including the domain name

- `smallimage`: The URL for the small image, not including the domain name

- `thumbnailspage`: The URL for the thumbnails page, not including the domain name

- `exif_model`: Information about camera model

- `exif_datetime`: The time the image was digitized

- `exif_exposuretime`: Exposure time

- `exif_fnumber`: The f-stop number

- `exif_isospeed`: ISO equivalent speed

- `exif_shutterspeed`: Shutter speed

- `exif_exposurebias`: The exposure bias used

- `exif_aperture`: The lens aperture

- `exif_meteringmode`: The camera metering mode

- `exif_flash`: Information about whether the flash was used

- `exif_focallength`: The focal length

- `keywords`: The keywords entered in the metadata form

Using the Thumbnail Template

Finally, the thumbnail template is usually similar to the index template but includes a full copy of the list of templates. The substitution variables are the same as the index template.

Conclusion

In this chapter, I presented a full demonstration of how to write a CGI and command-line application using Perl and ImageMagick's PerlMagick. In the next three chapters, I'll demonstrate three more examples of applications using ImageMagick—one in C, one in Ruby, and one in PHP. These demonstrations don't intend to show off all that is possible in these programming interfaces, as was done in the command-line discussion, but instead intend to present useful techniques and examples.

■■■

## CHAPTER 9

Implementing Your Own Delegate with C

This chapter is a slightly shorter example than the Perl example discussed in Chapter 8, although it still presents a useful tool to add to your ImageMagick arsenal. While writing the earlier chapters, I decided it would be useful to be able to implement support for other compression algorithms and file formats in ImageMagick, which is what this chapter demonstrates. Luckily for this chapter, ImageMagick has an extensible infrastructure, called *delegates*, for supporting image file formats. To implement a new file format, all you need to do is implement a new delegate.

How Delegates Are Configured

As mentioned in Chapter 1, you can configure delegates via the `delegates.xml` file. This file starts with this comment on its usage:

```
<!--

  Delegate command file.

  Commands which specify

    decode="in_format" encode="out_format"

  specify the rules for converting from in_format to out_format. These
  rules may be used to translate directly between formats.

  Commands which specify only

    decode="in_format"

  specify the rules for converting from in_format to some format which
  ImageMagick will automatically recognize. These rules are used to
  decode formats.
```

Commands which specify only

```
 encode="out_format"
```

specify the rules for an "encoder" which may accept any input format.

For delegates other than gs-color, gs-cmyk, gs-mono, pcl-color, pcl-cmyk, pcl-mono, and mpeg-encode, the substitution rules are as follows:

```
%i  input image filename
%o  output image filename
%u  unique temporary filename
%z  secondary unique temporary filename

%#  input image signature
%b  image file size
%c  input image comment
%g  window group
%h  image rows (height)
%k  input image number colors
%m  input image format
%p  page number
%q  input image depth
%s  scene number
%w  image columns (width)
%x  input image x resolution
%y  input image y resolution
```

```
-->
```

You can see from this that implementing a simple delegate isn't actually all that hard. For this example, I'll show how to write a delegate in a shell script that converts from a fictional file format called foo to PNG. It does this simply by copying the file (because foo files are really PNG files with a funny extension). Because of the simplistic nature of the delegate, the shell script is really simple:

```bash
#!/bin/bash

# This is a simple example of how to write a delegate in shell script
# It assumes the first argument is the input file and the second
# argument is the output file. It just renames the input to the output name.

cp $1 $2
```

Effectively, this is the smallest delegate possible. You also need to add the delegate to the delegates.xml configuration file. My configuration file looks like this once I add the new line:

```xml
<delegatemap>
    ...other delegates are registered here...
```

```
<delegate decode="foo" encode="png" mode="bi" ➥
command='"/home/mikal/imagemagickbook/delegate/simple.sh" "%i" "%o"' />
</delegatemap>
```

This configuration line says that to decode the foo format, use the command line specified, which will produce a PNG file. The command line specified uses a complete path to the simple shell script, passes the path to the input file as the first argument, and places a temporary path for output as the second argument. You don't need to specify a full path for the delegate executable if it's on the user's path.

Now, you can convert from the foo format to other formats like this:

```
convert input.foo output.tif
```

which will now perform as you would expect. If you want to encode to the foo format, then you merely need to reverse the values of the encode and decode parameters. Some additional options are available in the delegate's configuration file. The two most interesting are stealth mode, which stops the delegate from being listed by the list command-line argument to the convert command, and the spawn option, which forces the delegate to run in a new process, which means ImageMagick can continue executing once the delegate is started. This is useful for delegates that want to launch user interfaces, such as viewers. For these two options, the possible values are True and False.

Writing a Simple Delegate in C

Now it's time for a more complicated example using C. For this example, you could write lots of interesting delegates:

- You could have a database that stores images and want to use the images for other things. If the image filename was defined to be the unique identifier for the image in the database, and the images have a .db extension, then you could have a delegate that extracts the images from the database. This would make using these images as seamless to the user as if the images existed in the file system.

- You could write a delegate that extracts images from PDF files (not the whole page as an image but individual graphical elements) and places them in a multiple image format such as TIFF.

- A delegate to decode images that have been MIME encoded would be useful.

- Both the OV519 Web camera and the JVC car radio head unit in my car use image formats that aren't supported by ImageMagick. You could write delegates to support them.

For this chapter, I'll show how to write a simple delegate that renders black-and-white images to ASCII art. (The delegate could support color images, but you would need to convert them to grayscale before processing.) The rendering to ASCII art takes place with the aalib package, which can be found at http://aa-project.sf.net.

Additionally, because of the way aalib is intended to work, only relatively small images will work with this version of the delegate. You could improve this for future versions of the delegate, but I won't fix it here because it would complicate the example.

Without further ado, the following is the code for the delegate. The first argument it takes is the name of the input file, which must be a black-and-white TIFF image. The ASCII art is written to standard output, which means you'll need to redirect that in the delegate configuration.

```c
#include <stdio.h>
#include <unistd.h>
#include <string.h>
#include <stdlib.h>
#include <math.h>
#include <aalib.h>
#include <tiffio.h>

int
main (int argc, char **argv)
{
  int x, y, stripMax, stripCount, textwidth, xoffset, yoffset;
  TIFF *image;
  FILE *output;
  uint16 photo, bps, spp, fillorder;
  uint32 width, height;
  tsize_t stripSize;
  unsigned long imageOffset, result, bufferSize, count;
  char *text, *buffer, tempbyte;
  aa_context *context;
  aa_renderparams *params;

  // Open the TIFF image
  if ((image = TIFFOpen (argv[1], "r")) == NULL)
    {
      fprintf (stderr, "Could not open incoming image\n");
      exit (42);
    }

  // Open the output file
  output = fopen (argv[2], "w");
  fprintf (stderr, "Writing to %s\n", argv[2]);
  if (output == NULL)
    {
      fprintf (stderr, "Could not open output file\n");
      exit (42);
    }

  // Check that it is of a type that we support
  if ((TIFFGetField (image, TIFFTAG_BITSPERSAMPLE, &bps) == 0) || (bps != 1))
    {
```

```c
      fprintf (stderr,
               "Either undefined or unsupported number of bits per sample\n");
      exit (42);
    }

  if ((TIFFGetField (image, TIFFTAG_SAMPLESPERPIXEL, &spp) == 0)
      || (spp != 1))
    {
      fprintf (stderr,
               "Either undefined or unsupported number of samples per pixel\n");
      exit (42);
    }

  TIFFGetField (image, TIFFTAG_IMAGEWIDTH, &width);
  TIFFGetField (image, TIFFTAG_IMAGELENGTH, &height);

  // Initialize aalib, and ensure the image is blank
  context = aa_init (&mem_d, &aa_defparams, NULL);
  if (context == NULL)
    {
      fprintf (stderr, "Failed to initialize aalib\n");
      exit (1);
    }

  params = aa_getrenderparams ();

  memset (context->imagebuffer, 0,
          (size_t) (aa_imgwidth (context) * aa_imgheight (context)));

  // Check whether we can fit the image
  if (context->imgwidth < width)
    {
      fprintf (stderr,
               "Image too wide. It should be no more than %d pixels\n",
               context->imgwidth);
      exit (1);
    }
  if (context->imgheight < height)
    {
      fprintf (stderr,
               "Image too high. It should be no more than %d pixels\n\n",
               context->imgheight);
      exit (1);
    }
```

```
// Read in the possibly multiple strips
stripSize = TIFFStripSize (image);
stripMax = TIFFNumberOfStrips (image);
imageOffset = 0;

bufferSize = TIFFNumberOfStrips (image) * stripSize;
if ((buffer = (char *) malloc (bufferSize)) == NULL)
  {
    fprintf (stderr,
            "Could not allocate enough memory for the uncompressed image\n");
    exit (42);
  }

for (stripCount = 0; stripCount < stripMax; stripCount++)
  {
    if ((result = TIFFReadEncodedStrip (image, stripCount,
                                             buffer +
                                               imageOffset,
                                             stripSize)) == -1)
      {
          fprintf (stderr, "Read error on input strip number %d\n",stripCount);
          exit (42);
      }

    imageOffset += result;
  }

// Deal with photometric interpretations
if (TIFFGetField (image, TIFFTAG_PHOTOMETRIC, &photo) == 0)
  {
    fprintf (stderr, "Image has an undefined photometric interpretation\n");
    exit (42);
  }

if (photo != PHOTOMETRIC_MINISBLACK)
  {
    // Flip bits
    fprintf (stderr, "Fixing the photometric interpretation\n");

    for (count = 0; count < bufferSize; count++)
      buffer[count] = ~buffer[count];
  }

// Determine how to center the image
xoffset = (context->imgwidth - width) / 2;
yoffset = (context->imgheight - height) / 2;
```

```c
    // Copy the image across
    if (width % 8 != 0)
      width += (8 - width % 8);
    for (y = 0; y < height; y++)
      {
        for (x = 0; x < width / 8; x++)
          {
            if (((unsigned char) buffer[y * (width / 8) + x]) & 0x01)
              aa_putpixel (context, x * 8 + 7 + xoffset, y + yoffset, 255);
            if (((unsigned char) buffer[y * (width / 8) + x]) & 0x02)
              aa_putpixel (context, x * 8 + 6 + xoffset, y + yoffset, 255);
            if (((unsigned char) buffer[y * (width / 8) + x]) & 0x04)
              aa_putpixel (context, x * 8 + 5 + xoffset, y + yoffset, 255);
            if (((unsigned char) buffer[y * (width / 8) + x]) & 0x08)
              aa_putpixel (context, x * 8 + 4 + xoffset, y + yoffset, 255);

            if (((unsigned char) buffer[y * (width / 8) + x]) & 0x10)
              aa_putpixel (context, x * 8 + 3 + xoffset, y + yoffset, 255);
            if (((unsigned char) buffer[y * (width / 8) + x]) & 0x20)
              aa_putpixel (context, x * 8 + 2 + xoffset, y + yoffset, 255);
            if (((unsigned char) buffer[y * (width / 8) + x]) & 0x40)
              aa_putpixel (context, x * 8 + 1 + xoffset, y + yoffset, 255);
            if (((unsigned char) buffer[y * (width / 8) + x]) & 0x80)
              aa_putpixel (context, x * 8 + 0 + xoffset, y + yoffset, 255);
          }
      }

  aa_flush (context);
  aa_render (context, params, 0, 0,
             aa_imgwidth (context), aa_imgheight (context));

  text = strdup (aa_text (context));
  textwidth = aa_scrwidth (context);

  for (x = 0; x < strlen (text); x++)
    {
      fprintf (output, "%c", text[x]);
      if ((x + 1) % textwidth == 0)
        fprintf (output, "\n");
    }
  fprintf (output, "\n");

  TIFFClose (image);
  fclose (output);
  aa_close (context);
  return 0;
}
```

I won't describe the code in the commentary style I used in Chapter 8, because this code is a lot shorter. I'll briefly describe the flow of the program, though:

1. The program opens the TIFF image.

2. It opens the output file.

3. It ensures that the image is the right color depth.

4. It reads the size of the image.

5. aalib is initialized.

6. The maximum image size from aalib is compared to the size of the image.

7. The image is read into memory.

8. If the photometric interpretation (whether a zero is dark or light) is wrong, it's corrected.

9. The image offset to ensure centering is determined.

10. The image is drawn into the aalib buffer.

11. aalib is then asked to render the output, and that output is printed to the output file.

12. Everything is cleaned up.

As you can see, the most complicated parts of the whole process are reading the TIFF image in with libtiff and then ensuring that the image matches the supported image style for the delegate. Now you need to register the delegate with ImageMagick, like this:

```
<delegate decode="tiff" encode="aatext" mode="bi" ➥
command='"/home/mikal/imagemagickbook/delegate/aahelper" "%i" "%o"' />
```

Now that it's registered, you can convert images to ASCII art by using a command line like this:

```
convert input.tif output.aatext
```

For example, I'll show how to convert the image shown in Figure 9-1 to ASCII art.

Figure 9-1. *A sample input image*

You'll get the output (in a text file) shown in Figure 9-2.

```
QQQQQQQQQQQQQQf
QQQQQQQQQQQQQQf
QQQQQQQQQQQQQQf
QQQf   QQQf   QQQf
QQQf   QQQf   QQQf
QQQf   QQQf   QQQf
QQQf   QQQf   QQQf
QQQf   QQQf   QQQf
QQQf   QQQf   QQQf
QQQf   QQQf   QQQf
QQQbaaQQQbaaQQQf
QQQQQQQQQQQQQQf
QQQQQQQQQQQQQQf
QQQQQQQQQQQQQQf
    ]QQQQQQQQQQ
    ]QQQQQQQQQQ
aaJ??QQQQQP??aap
QQ[  QQQQQf  QQf
QQf  QQQQQf  QQf
QQQQQ      ]QQQf
QQQQQ      ]QQQf
QQQQQaaaaayQQQf
?????????????'
```

Figure 9-2. *A screen dump of a sample output image*

Conclusion

This chapter showed you a useful technique for implementing your own delegates. The next two chapters cover how to use Ruby and PHP with ImageMagick, both in the form of Web interfaces.

## CHAPTER 10

RMagick: ImageMagick Programming with Ruby

In this chapter, you'll examine a simple ImageMagick helper application written in Ruby using the RMagick Ruby interface for ImageMagick. The basic concept behind the application is that it's often easier to build a transformation of an image based on some simple visual steps and then apply those same transformations to several images. For example, I recently needed to take a large number of images, reduce their sizes, and then stamp them with a string before publishing them to a CD. At first this seemed like a trivial problem, but getting the images to look just right was much easier with the tool covered in this chapter. The script in this chapter is called imwizard. It's available for download from my site at http://www.stillhq.com/imagemagick/ruby/imwizard/.

Presenting the Code

The format for this chapter is similar to Chapter 8's coverage of PerlMagick. I'll present the code in an annotated format, and then I'll walk you through an example usage to make it clear how it works. Similar to Chapter 8, the code in this chapter is a simple sample implementation and by no means a complete example of how to use RMagick. The RMagick documentation at http://studio.imagemagick.org/RMagick/doc/index.html offers excellent help and is well worth a close look.

I'll now present the code for imwizard. This isn't a Ruby tutorial, but the following line tells the shell on Unix systems to run the Ruby interpreter in order to run this script:

```
#! /usr/bin/ruby -w
```

The following loads the RMagick Ruby interface to ImageMagick:

```
# Load the RMagick ImageMagick wrapper
require 'RMagick'
include Magick
```

The RMagick interface expects gravity to be expressed as an enumeration entry, but for this example you'll take a string from the user later in this script. The following function converts between the two by taking a string, running through the possible valid values, and returning the corresponding enumeration entry:

```ruby
# Convert a string to the right gravity enumeration entry
def togravity(str)
  case str
  when "Forget"
    return Magick::ForgetGravity
  when "NorthWest"
    return Magick::NorthWestGravity
  when "North"
    return Magick::NorthGravity
  when "NorthEast"
    return Magick::NorthEastGravity
  when "West"
    return Magick::WestGravity
  when "Center"
    return Magick::CenterGravity
  when "East"
    return Magick::EastGravity
  when "SouthWest"
    return Magick::SouthWestGravity
  when "South"
    return Magick::SouthGravity
  when "SouthEast"
    return Magick::SouthEastGravity
  else
    print "Unknown gravity\n"
    return Magick::Center
  end
end
```

The next function is where most of the work for the script is performed. It takes the following information: a command that the user entered, an image object (which is how RMagick passes around the state of an image), and whether to display the image after the transformation. This last parameter is because this function is used both when the user is interactively exploring a set of image transformations and when those transformations are being applied in a batch mode to a selection of images.

This function doesn't implement all the tasks you can do with RMagick—it implements only four commands to demonstrate what's possible. (Implementing more is left as an exercise for you.) Additionally, I avoid error checking in this code to make the ImageMagick operations clearer. Real code would, of course, include error checking.

```ruby
# Execute a command, either from the user or from the stored
# list of commands
def execute(execmd, oldimg, displayafter)
  cmdarray = execmd.split(" ")
  img = oldimg.dup
```

```ruby
  # To implement new commands, put them here...
  case cmdarray[0]
  when "annotate"
    text = Magick::Draw.new
    text.font = cmdarray[1]
    text.pointsize = cmdarray[2].to_i
    text.gravity = togravity(cmdarray[3])

    text.annotate(img, 0, 0, 0, 0, cmdarray[4]) {
      self.fill = cmdarray[5]
    }

  when "normalize"
    img = img.normalize

  when "resize"
    # The resize command destroys the aspect ratio of the image
    # so we do this instead
    img = img.change_geometry(cmdarray[1]){ |cols, rows, img|
      print "\t\tActual size: ", cols, "x", rows, "\n"
      img.resize!(cols, rows)
    }
```

The resize command can't just use the RMagick resize function, because that would affect the aspect ratio of the image (the ratio of the width of the image to the height of the image), so instead you ask RMagick to propose new dimensions that fit inside the user's passed geometry specification and then use those dimensions, as shown in the previous code.

```ruby
  when "spread"
    img = img.spread(cmdarray[1].to_i)

  else
    print "Command unknown\n"
    return img
  end

  if displayafter
  then
    img.display
  end
  return img
end
```

These are the commands implemented at the moment and the arguments they take:

annotate <fontname> <pointsize> <gravity> <text> <color>: Annotates the image with some text. annotate schmotto.ttf 30 SouthWest stillhq.com white is an example.

- `fontname`: The filename for a font to use.

- `pointsize`: The size of the text.

- `gravity`: The gravity to use for the text. The valid entries are listed in the `togravity` function shown previously.

- `text`: The text for the annotation.

- `color`: The color to use for the annotation.

`normalize`: Normalizes the image. This command takes no arguments.

`resize <geometry>`: Resizes the image. The geometry string used here is the same as those used for the various ImageMagick command-line tools. `resize 800x600` is an example.

`spread <radius>`: The same spread as the command-line option previously discussed in Chapter 5. This is the radius of the circle in which the pixel will be swapped. `spread 3` is an example.

When the script starts, it asks for an image to use for the example when the commands are being entered. This image is then loaded by RMagick and is immediately displayed to the user.

```
print "Welcome to imwizard. The basic flow works like this:\n"
print " - define an input filename\n\n"
print " - define an input pattern for the final application\n"
print " - try a command, the output is displayed\n"
print " - if you like that command, type \"commit\"\n"
print " - otherwise try another command\n\n"
print "When you're finished, type done\n"
print "Type help for help\n\n"

print "input filename >> "
input = gets.chomp
print "Loading image...\n"
img = ImageList.new(input)
img.display
print "Done\n\n"
```

`imwizard` builds an array of commands that have been committed. Once this array has been prepared, you start reading commands from standard input.

```
cmds = Array.new
prevcmd = ""
newimg = img

while true
  print ">> "
  cmd = gets.chomp

  case cmd
```

The first command, help, is a simple online help system. It documents the commands described previously.

```
when "help"
  print "\n"
  print "You can enter a command here, commit a command, or end.\n"
  print "The commit a command, type the word commit on a line by itself.\n"
  print "To end, type done on a line by itself\n\n"
  print "Valid commands are:\n\n"
  print "\tannotate <fontname> <pointsize> <gravity> <text> <color>\n"
  print "\tnormalize\n"
  print "\tresize <geometry>\n"
  print "\tspread <radius>\n"
  print "\n\n"
```

When the user is finished playing with commands and wants to implement the changes for a set of images, they execute the done command. This results in them being prompted for a path to the images to change and a regular expression describing those images. Those images then have the commands previously committed executed against them, and the changed image is saved over the original image.

```
when "done"
    print "Now you need to tell me where to implement the changes.\n"
    print "path >> "
    path = gets.chomp
    print "Now I need a regular expression which defines the images to change\n"
    print "regexp >> "
    re = gets.chomp

    print "Processing...\n"
    Dir.foreach(path) do |file|
      regexp = Regexp.new(re)
      match = regexp.match(file)
      if match
      then
        print "Processing ", file, "\n"
        img = ImageList.new(path + "/" + file)
        cmds.each do |cmd|
          img = execute(cmd, img, false)
        end
        img.write(path + "/" + file)
      end
    end
    print "Bye\n"
    exit
```

For each command executed, the user needs to commit that command if they're happy with it, as follows. If the command isn't committed, then it's ignored and not added to the list of commands to batch execute.

```
when "commit"
  if prevcmd != ""
  then
    cmds.push(prevcmd)
    img = newimg
    prevcmd = ""
    print cmds.join("\n"), "\n"
  else
    print "There is nothing to commit...\n"
  end
```

Otherwise, you can assume this is a command that changes the image and tries to execute it.

```
  else
    prevcmd = cmd
    newimg = execute(cmd, img, true)
  end
end

exit
```

Seeing the Helper Application in Action

In this section, I'll walk you through a complete example of the execution of the script, including sample images. In the following output, bold text indicates text entered by the user:

./imwizard

```
Welcome to imwizard. The basic flow works like this:
 - define an input filename

 - define an input pattern for the final application
 - try a command, the output is displayed
 - if you like that command, type "commit"
 - otherwise try another command

When you're finished, type done
Type help for help

input filename >> input.jpg
Loading image...
Done
```

The input image will now be displayed to the user. The input image I'll use as an example looks like Figure 10-1.

Figure 10-1. *The input image for this example*

Please note that this image has been scaled to fit on the page. You can resize images with imwizard, like so:

```
>> resize 10x10
            Actual size: 10x7
```

The user now sees a 10×7-pixel version of the image, as shown in Figure 10-2.

Figure 10-2. *A tiny image*

Let's say the user regrets making the image this small, so they don't commit the change. Instead, they retry the command, as follows:

```
>> resize 800x800
            Actual size: 800x533
```

This returns the bigger image shown in Figure 10-3.

Figure 10-3. *A bigger image*

The user then decides that this is the right image and commits the command, as shown here:

```
>> commit
resize 800x800
```

The line of text at the end of this command is a list of the commands that have been committed.

The user then decides to annotate the image with a domain name so that people know where the image originated:

```
>> annotate schmotto.ttf 30 SouthWest stillhq.com white
>> commit
resize 800x800
annotate schmotto.ttf 30 SouthWest stillhq.com white
```

The user will now see an annotated version of the image, as shown in Figure 10-4, and then this command is committed as well, which results in two commands appearing in the list of committed commands.

Figure 10-4. *A bigger image with an annotation*

When the user is finished entering commands, they type the done command, as shown here:

>> **done**

They're then prompted for a path to the images to process, as well as a regular expression that defines the images to process. I'll show how to process all the images in the photos/mikal directory that have filenames ending in .jpg:

```
Now you need to tell me where to implement the changes.
path >> photos/mikal
Now I need a regular expression that defines the images to change
regexp >> ^.*\.jpg$
```

The processing now begins:

```
Processing...
Processing 100_LCA.jpg
                Actual size: 800x600
Processing 101_LCA.jpg
                Actual size: 800x600
Processing 102_LCA.jpg
                Actual size: 600x800
Processing 103_LCA.jpg
                Actual size: 800x499
Processing 104_LCA.jpg
                Actual size: 800x600
Processing 105_LCA.jpg
                Actual size: 800x600
Processing 106_LCA.jpg
                Actual size: 800x600
Processing 107_LCA.jpg
                Actual size: 800x600
Processing 108_LCA.jpg
                Actual size: 600x800
Processing 109_LCA.jpg
                Actual size: 453x800
Processing 110_LCA.jpg
                Actual size: 800x600
Processing 111_LCA.jpg
```

And so on:

```
Bye
```

The code will say "Bye" when it has finished processing.

Conclusion

In this chapter, you saw an example of how to use ImageMagick with the RMagick Ruby interface. I showed you how to write a helper application that assists the user in deciding which transformations to apply to a group of images and then applies those transformations to the selected set of images. The sample application in this chapter was by no means complete, but it shows you the skeletal structure of what a more complete application would look like, without a lot of code getting in the way. Note that the Ruby programming language provides an expressive, powerful interface to ImageMagick, without bogging you down with having to write a lot of code.

In the remaining two chapters of the book, you'll examine one last programming interface—this time for PHP—and then find out where to go from what's covered in this book.

## CHAPTER 11

MagickWand: ImageMagick Programming with PHP

In this chapter, I'll discuss the MagickWand interface to the PHP Web programming language. Instead of showing off how to manipulate existing images, do something artistic, or perform anything like that (all of which is possible with MagickWand), I'll show you how to create dynamic graphics for a hypothetical Web application.

Presenting the Problem

Imagine that you're writing a Web application that automates the process of rental property management—landlords can register properties and then keep track of the administration of their properties. Tenants can use the site to find properties to rent, apply for properties they like, make rental payments, and so on. The problem is that the site isn't very visually appealing, and it lacks visualization tools. I'll show you how to fix that by adding some dynamic graphs to the site.

The sample I'll use in this chapter is a graph of rental property values for a specific region. When a landlord is picking the price they would like to charge, the site will display a graph of rental properties in a similar region matching the description of the property that the landlord entered. The landlord can then make an informed decision about what to charge for their property, based on the dominant market trends.

The Web site needs to generate these graphs, and the developer has decided to do that with ImageMagick. It's a PHP site, so therefore the logical choice is to use MagickWand.

Presenting the Implementation

I'll discuss a few aspects of implementing the graph before presenting the PHP code. The graph is a separate element of the HTML page that the PHP application generates, just as it would be for any other Web site. The Web page that shows the graph looks like Figure 11-1.

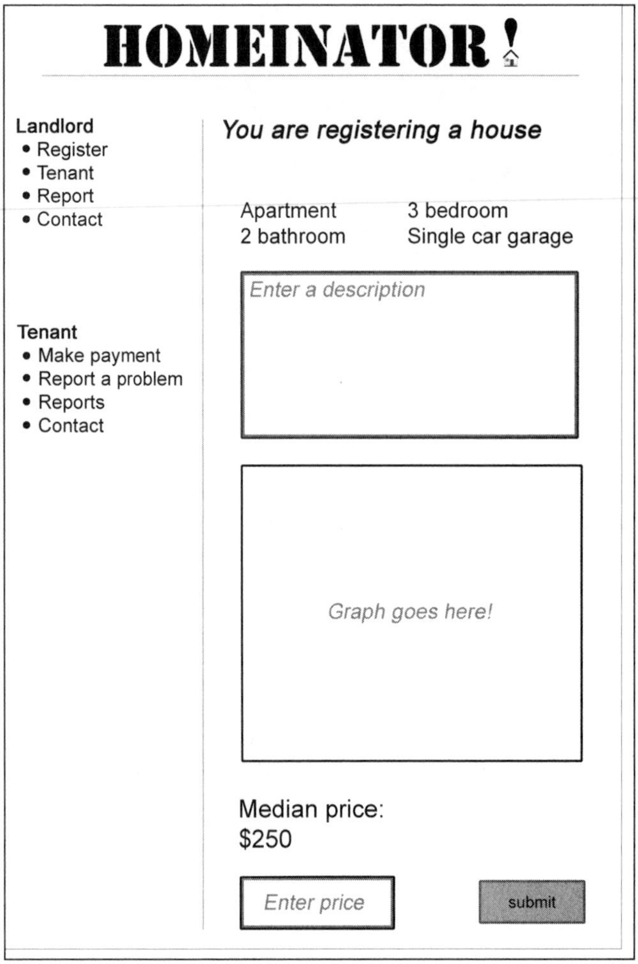

Figure 11-1. *A Web page containing the graph*

You can see the graph in the middle of the page. Rhys Jones from http://www.rustybones.net kindly created this HTML page (because Web site design is unfortunately not one of my talents!).

The graph is linked to this page with an IMG tag that looks something like this:

```
<img src="/images/graph.php?suburb=gordon">
```

This link is important, because it means the graphing code is decoupled from the HTML page shown in Figure 11-1; in fact, it's embedded in an entirely other PHP page. In fact, no HTML appears in the graphing code, just the PHP to generate the graph.

Creating a Background Image

The technique to implement the graph involves laying the graph elements on top of a standard background image. This image will contain the axes for the graph, the scale, a key, and some descriptive text. Figure 11-2 shows the background image I'll use for this example.

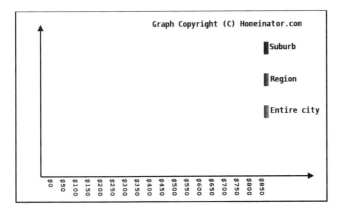

Figure 11-2. *The background image for the graph*

This makes it really easy to change much of the style of the graph without having to change any code.

Creating the Bar Images

I'll also use three other images to make the graphs. These images are stacked to form the bars in the bar graph. They have three styles, because the graph has three sets of values. Figure 11-3, Figure 11-4, and Figure 11-5 show the zoomed-in forms of these images.

Figure 11-3. *A red image to build bars from, zoomed in*

Figure 11-4. *A green image to build bars from, zoomed in*

Figure 11-5. *A blue image to build bars from, zoomed in*

These images will look fairly similar because of the grayscale printing process used for this book, but they're actually quite different in real life. These three images make the final graphs, which look like Figure 11-6.

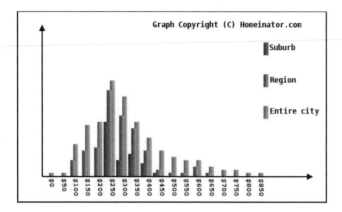

Figure 11-6. *A sample output graph*

Presenting the Code

This section presents the code that produces this graph. The following utility function loads the bar images for you:

```
<?
  #############################################################################
  # Utility functions
  #############################################################################


  # This function reads in an image and returns it, including error handling.
  function readimage($filename)
  {
    $barhandle = imagick_readimage($filename);
    if(imagick_iserror($barhandle))
    {
      $reason      = imagick_failedreason($barhandle);
      $description = imagick_faileddescription($barhandle);

      print "handle failed!<BR>\nReason: $reason<BR>\n➥
        Description: $description<BR>\n";
      exit ;
    }
```

```
  $img = imagick_getimagefromlist($barhandle);
  imagick_destroyhandle($barhandle);
  return $img;
}
```

Next you'll see the main code for the graph. The background image is loaded.

```
# Read in the image for the background to the graph
$handle = imagick_readimage(getcwd() . "/graph.png");
if(imagick_iserror($handle))
{
  $reason      = imagick_failedreason($handle);
  $description = imagick_faileddescription($handle);

  print "handle failed!<BR>\nReason: $reason<BR>\nDescription: $description<BR>\n";
  exit ;
}
```

The colored bar images are loaded using that helper function from earlier:

```
# Read in the images we use to draw the bars. There are three of them -- a red bar,
# a blue bar, and a green bar
$redbar = readimage(getcwd() . "/redbar.png");
$greenbar = readimage(getcwd() . "/greenbar.png");
$bluebar = readimage(getcwd() . "/bluebar.png");
```

The following code is a stub. Normally you'd need to fetch the values from some form of database, but because this book is about ImageMagick and not about working with databases and PHP, I've omitted that code for clarity.

You have to set up three arrays: match contains how many houses match the description, broken into price brackets; region contains a similar list but for the area the suburb is in; and finally city is a similar list for the entire city.

```
# Now fetch the data from the database (this is a simulated fetch only).
# Let's assume that there are three sets of data we want to show --
# houses which match this description, houses in this suburb, and
# houses in this region...
# ...
$max = 18;
```

The following code actually creates the graph. It uses the ImageMagick composite functionality to place copies of the bar strips onto the background image to create the graph. Each array is handled separately here.

```
# The graphing for the moment assumes that the maximum value to be graphed is small
# enough that we should give each increase of one in the input value an extra five
# rows in the graph
for($i = 0; $i < $max; $i++)
{
  for($j = 0; $j < $city[$i] * 5; $j++)
```

```
    {
      imagick_composite($handle, IMAGICK_COMPOSITE_OP_OVER,
        $greenbar, 42 + 10 + ($i * 20), 259 - $j);
    }
}

for($i = 0; $i < $max; $i++)
{
  for($j = 0; $j < $region[$i] * 5; $j++)
  {
    imagick_composite($handle, IMAGICK_COMPOSITE_OP_OVER,
      $redbar, 42 + 5 + ($i * 20), 259 - $j);
  }
}

for($i = 0; $i < $max; $i++)
{
  for($j = 0; $j < $match[$i] * 5; $j++)
  {
    imagick_composite($handle, IMAGICK_COMPOSITE_OP_OVER,
      $bluebar, 42 + ($i * 20), 259 - $j);
  }
}
```

Finally, you can ask MagickWand to put the image into a variable, which you can then output to the browser by printing it. The header line here is important, because otherwise the browser will not know how to interpret the data returned. The arguments to the imagemagick_composite function consist of the following: the image handle, the composite operation as discussed in Chapter 7, the image handle for the image to place onto the first image handle, and the x and y coordinates for the top-left placement.

```
  # This dumps the image to a variable, so that we can output it to the
  #  browser
  if(!$dump = imagick_image2blob($handle))
  {
    $reason      = imagick_failedreason($handle);
    $description = imagick_faileddescription($handle);

    print "imagick_writeimage() failed<BR>\nReason: $reason<BR>\n➡
      Description: $description<BR>\n";
    exit ;
  }

  # Output the finished graph to the browser
  header("Content-Type: image/jpeg");
  print $dump;
?>
```

Conclusion

In this chapter, you learned that it's relatively trivial to create good-looking, dynamic graphs with ImageMagick in PHP. This chapter (and the previous three) covered four common programming problems with ImageMagick in four common languages. The next chapter of the book will show where to get more support for ImageMagick and cover how to become an active member of the ImageMagick community.

CHAPTER 12

■ ■ ■

Where to Go from Here

I've covered a lot of ground in this book, including how to install ImageMagick, how to use almost all the functionality of the command-line utilities that ImageMagick ships with, and how to program against four of ImageMagick's APIs. No book can cover all the questions you could ask, though—perhaps some are so unique they're not of general interest, perhaps the ImageMagick software has moved on since the printing of this book, or perhaps I just didn't think of your specific question when I was writing the manuscript!

Where Do You Find Help Online?

Don't let your experience with ImageMagick stop here, though. If you find a flaw with this book, or an omission, then please refer to my ImageMagick blog at `http://www.stillhq.com/imagemagick/` or the Web site for the book at `http://www.apress.com/book/bookDisplay.html?bID=10052`. Failing that, let me know by sending e-mail to `imagemagick@stillhq.com`.

For more generic answers and help with ImageMagick, you should investigate the wealth of resources that are available for ImageMagick on the Internet. The first stop for information about ImageMagick should be the ImageMagick Web site at `http://www.imagemagick.org`. There you'll find links to ImageMagick tutorials, documentation, and information on the ImageMagick mailing lists and forums. At the time of writing, you can find the mailing lists at `http://www.imagemagick.org/script/mailing-list.php`.

Several mailing lists exist for ImageMagick discussions:

- *magick-users*: This list is for discussion amongst the users of ImageMagick, although members of the development team hang out here as well. The intention is that this list is used for people to ask questions, which are answered by other members of the list.

- *magick-developers*: This is where the programmers who work on ImageMagick talk. If you want to get involved in the development of ImageMagick, or just want a feel for what's going on and what's coming up, this is the place to be.

- *magick-bugs*: This is where to report bugs.

- *magick-announce*: This is the low-traffic list that announces new releases.

Searching the mailing list archives, which are linked from `http://www.imagemagick.org/script/mailing-list.php`, is a really useful technique for finding answers for your questions without having to ask the questions on the list. It's generally a good idea to search the archives first, because list members get frustrated if the same questions are asked repeatedly.

Other sites are useful to users of ImageMagick as well. Internet searching will produce many tutorials and examples that are relevant to various aspects of ImageMagick. Probably the most complete online tutorial for ImageMagick is by Anthony Thyssen at `http://www.cit.gu.edu.au/~anthony/graphics/imagick6/`. This excellent tutorial works through many ImageMagick features, although it's not yet complete.

What If You Find a Bug in ImageMagick?

In the unlikely event that you find a bug in ImageMagick, then you should follow certain steps to help resolve the issue. The first is to make sure you're using the most recent version of ImageMagick. This is especially true if you're using an older version of an operating system or if you have used packages provided by your operating system vendor. Regardless, refer to `http://www.imagemagick.org` to ensure you are running the latest version of the package.

Next, you should make sure the bug hasn't already been reported. This helps the ImageMagick developers, because it stops them from having to handle repeated requests (perhaps while trying to work on a fix for your problem); additionally, the previous bug report might have already documented a fix for the problem. ImageMagick doesn't have a bug tracker, although it's worthwhile to check the ImageMagick developer mailing list (as described earlier) to see whether your problem has already been discussed.

Many operating system vendors also have excellent bug-reporting facilities, and it's possible that the bug is being tracked in their systems. For example, I use Debian Linux for a lot of my work, and the Debian bug tracker is excellent. You can find all known Debian bugs for ImageMagick at `http://bugs.debian.org/cgi-bin/pkgreport.cgi?which=pkg&data=imagemagick&➡archive=no&version=&dist=unstable`. Other operating system vendors have similar facilities.

If you haven't been able to find a resolution to your problem, then the next step is to e-mail the magick-bugs mailing list at `magick-bugs@imagemagick.org`. This message should include a brief but complete description of the bug and any information needed to re-create the bug on a developer's machine. This will include facts such as the command line or code you were executing and links to the input images you were using at the time.

Finally, at some stage, a fix for your problem will become available, and you'll be asked to test the fix and confirm that it works for you. This is an important part of the process, because it tells the developers they are on the right track.

Similarly, if you fix the bug yourself, then e-mail the magick-developers mailing list at `magick-developers@imagemagick.org` and include details of the bug and the changes you made to the code, as described by the `diff` program.

Conclusion

ImageMagick is an incredibly powerful package with a large number of options. I cover the most important options in this book, providing a useful guide to the package. In this chapter, I filled in a few blanks by discussing online resources for ImageMagick and by describing how to join the ImageMagick community by subscribing to the ImageMagick mailing lists. Enjoy your travels with ImageMagick!

Index

Y

YUV, website address for information about, 66
YUV color space, image information in,
        65–66

 Z

zip compression, 61
zlib delegate, website address for
        downloading, 10

forums.apress.com

JOIN THE APRESS FORUMS AND BE PART OF OUR COMMUNITY. You'll find discussions that cover topics of interest to IT professionals, programmers, and enthusiasts just like you. If you post a query to one of our forums, you can expect that some of the best minds in the business—especially Apress authors, who all write with *The Expert's Voice*™—will chime in to help you. Why not aim to become one of our most valuable participants (MVPs) and win cool stuff? Here's a sampling of what you'll find:

DATABASES

Data drives everything.

Share information, exchange ideas, and discuss any database programming or administration issues.

INTERNET TECHNOLOGIES AND NETWORKING

Try living without plumbing (and eventually IPv6).

Talk about networking topics including protocols, design, administration, wireless, wired, storage, backup, certifications, trends, and new technologies.

JAVA

We've come a long way from the old Oak tree.

Hang out and discuss Java in whatever flavor you choose: J2SE, J2EE, J2ME, Jakarta, and so on.

MAC OS X

All about the Zen of OS X.

OS X is both the present and the future for Mac apps. Make suggestions, offer up ideas, or boast about your new hardware.

OPEN SOURCE

Source code is good; understanding (open) source is better.

Discuss open source technologies and related topics such as PHP, MySQL, Linux, Perl, Apache, Python, and more.

PROGRAMMING/BUSINESS

Unfortunately, it is.

Talk about the Apress line of books that cover software methodology, best practices, and how programmers interact with the "suits."

WEB DEVELOPMENT/DESIGN

Ugly doesn't cut it anymore, and CGI is absurd.

Help is in sight for your site. Find design solutions for your projects and get ideas for building an interactive Web site.

SECURITY

Lots of bad guys out there—the good guys need help.

Discuss computer and network security issues here. Just don't let anyone else know the answers!

TECHNOLOGY IN ACTION

Cool things. Fun things.

It's after hours. It's time to play. Whether you're into LEGO® MINDSTORMS™ or turning an old PC into a DVR, this is where technology turns into fun.

WINDOWS

No defenestration here.

Ask questions about all aspects of Windows programming, get help on Microsoft technologies covered in Apress books, or provide feedback on any Apress Windows book.

HOW TO PARTICIPATE:

Go to the Apress Forums site at **http://forums.apress.com/**.

Click the New User link.

```
mogrify -crop 2040x1530+820+200! -rsize 50% -rotate 90 *.jpg
              xdim ydim xUL yUL
```